Basic English Usage
Exercises

Jennifer Seidl
Michael Swan

Oxford University Press

Oxford University Press
Walton Street, Oxford OX2 6DP

Oxford   New York   Toronto
Delhi   Bombay   Calcutta   Madras   Karachi
Petaling Jaya   Singapore   Hong Kong   Tokyo
Nairobi   Dar es Salaam   Cape Town
Melbourne   Auckland

and associated companies in
Beirut   Berlin   Ibadan   Nicosia

OXFORD is a trade mark of Oxford University Press.

ISBN 0 19 431188 0

© Oxford University Press 1986

First published 1986
Second impression 1986

Cartoons by Marie-Hélène Jeeves
Other illustrations by Katey Farrell, Alan Suttie
Photographs by Rob Judges, Terry Williams

The publishers would like to thank Hertz, Daimler-
Benz AG, British Telecom and the International Wool
Secretariat for permission to use trade marks and
copyright material, and Barnabys, Camera Press, Rex
Features for permission to reproduce photographs.

Typeset by Tradespools Ltd, Frome, Somerset

Printed in Hong Kong

Contents

Introduction

General

This book of exercises was written to accompany Michael Swan's *Basic English Usage*, but it can also be used on its own. It provides practice and revision material on over 200 important points of usage, grammar and lexis. It is intended for students of English from lower intermediate level upwards and is suitable both for use in class and for self study.

Exercises

The 230 exercises are varied in approach to suit the topic and the needs of the user. With few exceptions, the exercises are contextualized. Many exercises make use of picture cues. Several exercises are controlled, i.e. they have a limited number of possible answers. Others are open-ended, i.e. they offer freer communicative practice. Here the student is guided towards expressing wishes, preferences, opinions, etc within the framework of a specific language item. The student relates to and draws on his personal situation, own background and experience.

Organization

The language points treated are dealt with alphabetically, as in *Basic English Usage*. In the vast majority of cases, each exercise deals with one *BEU* point only. This makes the exercise book very easy to use together with *Basic English Usage*. All exercises are cross-referenced to the corresponding sections of *Basic English Usage* and most have at least one example.

Key

There is a full Key for students working on their own. Where the exercise is open-ended, suggestions are made or examples of possible answers are given.

List of Exercises

1 about to (BEU 2)

What are they all about to do?

▶ *The policeman's **about to** stop the traffic.* (1)

1

2

3

4

5

6

7

8

9

10

11

2 **above** and **over** (BEU 3)

above, *over* or both?

I'm a student and I have a room in London. The house is __1__ a hundred years old, so my room's cheap but shabby. In the corner there's a bed with a red cover __2__ it. __3__ the bed there's a shelf for books. There's a crack in the wall __4__ the fire-place, so I've stuck a poster __5__ it. Just __6__ the crack there's a hole, so I've put a photo of my girlfriend __7__ that. There's a broken mirror __8__ the wash-basin, and just __9__ that there's a light that doesn't work. But the room's wonderful for parties! Last night I had __10__ twenty friends here. It really doesn't matter if anything gets broken!

3 **across, over, through** (BEU 4, 5)

across, *over* or *through*?

We live in a farmhouse in the country. When you get off the bus, you have to walk __1__ the village, __2__ the square, __3__ the narrow streets and __4__ the market-place to the church. Then you turn left and go __5__ the bridge. Don't jump __6__ the stream – it's deep! Walk __7__ the wood and __8__ the ploughed field. There's a fence round it, but you can jump __9__ that. You'll see the farmhouse from the top of the hill. If the gate's locked, just climb __10__ the wall – I always do.

4 adverbs: position (BEU 14)

Copy the story, putting the adverbs in the correct position.

```
                          7

 certainly ─────→ She glanced at her watch - 2.30 am. But      completely
                  it had been a lovely party. She had for-
                  gotten the time. She turned the key in        quietly
                  the door. But how strange - it wasn't         even
          really  locked. Had she forgotten to lock the
          perhaps door? She had. A strange feeling came         nevertheless
         suddenly over her. Her heart started beating. She      loudly
        nervously pushed the door open and listened. She
         upstairs heard a noise. It had come from the bed-      definitely
         at first  room. She didn't know what to do. There
        obviously  was someone in the house. She must think     clearly
                   what to do. She knew that she must ring
         at once   the police. She moved towards the phone.     silently
           then    She remembered that it was out of order.
                                                                the morning
                   She had tried to phone her brother.          before
   unfortunately
                   She groped her way back to the door. There
                   was a china vase. She brushed against it     on the hall
                                                                table
```

5 adverbs: indefinite frequency (BEU 14.2)

What's the weather like? Answer these questions
about the weather in your country.
Use: *always*, *never*, *often*, *sometimes*, *occasionally*
and *rarely* in complete sentences.

▶ Is it hot in summer?
*Yes, it's **always** hot in summer.*

Is there snow in August?
*No, there's **never** snow in August.*

1 Is there ever snow in winter?
2 Is it ever foggy?
3 Is there heavy rainfall in summer?
4 Is it ever hotter than 30°C?
5 Are there ever thunderstorms?
6 Can you sunbathe in winter?
7 Is it humid?
8 Is the temperature ever below freezing point?
9 Are there ever floods?
10 Is there ever a hurricane in your area?

6 adverbs: indefinite frequency (BEU 14.2)

What do you do in your free time? Say:

▶ what you *often* do on Saturdays.
*On Saturdays I **often** go shopping.*

1 what you *always* do on Sundays. (Begin: *On
Sundays I **always** . . .*)
2 what you *often* do after school/work.
3 what you *seldom* do during the week.
4 what you *never* do at weekends.

5 what you *frequently* do in summer.
6 what you *rarely* do in winter.
7 what you *sometimes* do on holiday.
8 what you *usually* do on Sunday mornings.
9 what you *normally* do when it rains.
10 what you *occasionally* do in the evenings.

7 adverbs of manner (BEU 14.6)

Answer these questions about yourself.

▶ Are you a good swimmer?
*Yes, I swim **well**.*
*No, I don't swim **well**./No, I
swim **badly**.*

1 Are you a good cook?
2 Are you a hard worker?
3 Are you a fast learner?
4 Are you a fluent speaker
of English?
5 Are you a good singer?

6 Are you a heavy smoker?
7 Are you a fast runner?
8 Are you a good dancer?
9 Are you a careful driver?
10 Are you a good tennis player?

8 adverbs: position (place, time) (BEU 14.9)

What's Jill doing this week?

▶ *She has to ring Jim at his office at lunchtime.*

Continue . . .

```
                              ❀NOTES❀
Today
ring Jim lunchtime (office)
see Brenda 12.30 (canteen)
2.15 dentist's
5.30 pick up Roger, Kings Cross
                              Station
7.30 jazz concert, Cavern Club
```

```
                              ❀NOTES❀
Tues
afternoon, town with Sarah
disco 8pm
Wed
9.15 interview, Sun Travel Agency
8pm Central Hall, concert
Thurs Manchester, 8.15 am.
meet Sally about 6.30pm, airport
```

9 after (preposition); afterwards (adverb) (BEU 16)

What did the Parkers do in London?

▶ *On Monday morning . . .* **after** *visiting St. Paul's Cathedral, they took a walk through the City.*
or
they visited St. Paul's Cathedral and **afterwards** *they took a walk through the City.*

Continue . . .

London, August 17–20

Mon 17: St. Paul's Cathedral
Morn. walk through city

aft. Westminster Abbey; Houses of Parliament

even. The Mousetrap (Agatha Christie), Chinese restaurant

Tues 18: Madame Tussaud's;
Morn the Planetarium

aft. Windsor Castle walk through Windsor

even. boat ride on the Thames Meal at steak House

Wed 19: shopping — Oxford Street
morn. lunch Italian restaurant

aft. British Museum; a few beers in a nearby pub

even. concert, Queen Elizabeth Hall, supper Indian restaurant

Thurs 20: 10 Downing Street,
Morn. Hyde Park

aft. Tate Gallery coffee-shop

even. packed suit-cases

10 ago (BEU 20)

ago, for or *before*?

1981: waiter, building site	1982: office job, waiter
1983: tourist guide	1984: office job, building site

In summer 1984, last year, I did an office job __1__ six weeks. I knew the work because I had done it two years __2__ . Two years __3__ , in summer 1983, I worked as a tourist guide in London __4__ three months. In summer 1982, that's three years __5__ , I also worked as a waiter in a London hotel. I had already been a waiter __6__ three months a year __7__ , so it wasn't new to me. A year __8__ , I also worked on a building site __9__ four weeks. I had worked for the same firm three years __10__ .

11 all (BEU 21–24)

all, everybody, everything, every?

POLICEMAN   Now, please tell me __1__ you know, Madam.
MRS YOUNG   Well, when I came downstairs this morning I switched on __2__ the lights, and __3__ was in a mess! __4__ the silver was missing, pictures, money, __5__ my jewellery. They had taken __6__ ! They had been in __7__ drawer and cupboard.

POLICEMAN   Where was __8__ at the time?
MRS YOUNG   In bed, of course, we were __9__ asleep.
POLICEMAN   Did the neighbours hear or see anything?
MRS YOUNG   __10__ our neighbours are on holiday. __11__ goes away at this time of the year.
POLICEMAN   All right, Madam. I'll just take a look round. Thank you. That's __12__ for now.

12 **although** (BEU 29)

Rewrite with *although*.

▶ I don't sleep much, but I'm not usually tired.
   ***Although** I don't sleep much, I'm not usually tired.*

1 I eat a lot, but I'm not fat.
2 I get up late, but I'm seldom late for work.
3 I drink a lot of beer, but I'm never drunk.
4 I drive badly, but I've never had an accident.
5 I don't look after my car, but it runs well.
6 I spend a lot of money, but I'm not in debt.
7 I don't go to the dentist's, but my teeth are healthy.

Write about some of your bad habits. Use *although*.

13 **another** (BEU 33)

You are invited to tea with an English family. How would you ask for *another* or *some more* of the following things?
Begin: *May/Could I have... , please?*

cup of tea	piece of chocolate cake
sugar	apple pie
sandwich	cream
two biscuits	piece of fruit cake
milk	strawberry gâteau

14 articles: **the**, **a/an** (BEU 40, 41)

the or *a*?

POLLY   There are two people sitting near __1__ door, __2__ young man and __3__ woman. __4__ man's wearing __5__ dark raincoat and __6__ woman's got __7__ big, black bag. They look suspicious. They are watching __8__ bank across __9__ road. And there's __10__ man standing at __11__ entrance to __12__ bank...

ALICE   Do you mean __13__ man in __14__ black hat?
POLLY   Yes, he looks very suspicious.
ALICE   Well, stop playing detective and pass me __15__ sugar, please. I know him – he's __16__ bank manager!

15 articles: special rules and exceptions (BEU 45)

Answer these questions about yourself. Write complete sentences, and put in *the* if necessary.

▶ What time do you go to ____ work?
   I go to work at eight o'clock.

   Do you live in ____ town or in ____ country?
   *I live in **the** country.*

1 What time do you go to ____ work?
2 Do you live in ____ town or in ____ country?
3 What do you eat for ____ breakfast?
4 Do you go to school/work by ____ bus, by ____ bicycle or on ____ foot?
5 Do you play ____ piano or ____ guitar?
6 Do you prefer ____ mountains or ____ sea?
7 Do you prefer to go on holiday in ____ spring or in ____ summer?
8 Do you often lie in ____ sun?
9 Have you ever been in ____ hospital?
10 How often do you watch ____ television?

16 articles: special rules and exceptions (BEU 45)

Answer these questions about your country or your town. Use *the* or no article.

▶ 1 **The** Amazon
   2 *Rio Airport*

1 Which is the longest river?
2 Which is the main airport?
3 Which is the biggest lake?
4 Which are the nearest mountains?
5 Which is the highest mountain?

6 Which is the nearest sea or ocean?
7 Which is the biggest or most important university?
8 Which is the main street in your town?
9 Which is the biggest hotel in your town?
10 Which is the nearest railway station?

17 articles: **a/an** (BEU 45.6)

What are they?

translator	electrician	author	mechanic
air hostess	secretary	architect	shop assistant
nurse	actor		

▶ *Ann's **a** secretary.*

	Ann	Pam	Mike	Jim	Jeff	Joe	Pat	Bill	Tom	Mark
works in an office	●					●			●	
sells things										●
repairs things				●	●					
uses languages		●							●	
types a lot	●		●						●	
visits customers					●	●				
works with others	●	●		●			●	●		●
sometimes works at night		●					●	●		
has a famous name			●					●		

18 **as . . . as** (BEU 46)

Compare using *as . . . as* and *not as . . . as*.

▶ Jim's 16, Ben's 18 and Jack's 16.
   *Jim's **as old as** Jack, but he isn't **as old as** Ben.*

1 Mary's 160 cm tall, Pat's 160 cm and Pam's 172 cm tall.
2 Dick smokes 25 cigarettes a day, Tom 40 and Peter 25.
3 Susan works 8 hours a day, Jane 8 hours and Jill 10 hours.
4 Peter earns £160 a week, Dick earns £160 and Tom earns £190.

5 Uncle Stan weighs 88 kilos, Uncle Sam weighs 108 kilos and Uncle Dan weighs 88 kilos.
6 Susan gets up at 7.30, Jill at 6.30 and Jane at 7.30.

Write some sentences like these to compare yourself with other people.

19 **as** and **like** (BEU 48)

as or *like*?

1 You look very much _____ someone I know.
2 I worked _____ a tour guide in London for three months.
3 Mr Turner is really very nice. You don't know him _____ I do.
4 Peter can swim _____ a fish!
5 I like travelling in hot countries, _____ Nigeria or Pakistan.
6 I'm good at some things, _____ music and painting.
7 In Spain, _____ in several hot countries, shops close for a few hours around midday.
8 Polly tries to dress _____ a model, but she doesn't look quite the same.
9 This year, _____ last year, all evening classes will begin at 7.30 pm.
10 Don't try to change anything. Leave things _____ they are.

20 **as, when** and **while** (BEU 52.1)

Find beginnings and ends that go together. Begin with *as*, *when* or *while*.

▶ **As/When/While** *I was hanging out the washing, it started to rain.*

Beginnings
I was cleaning the floor
I was phoning my aunt
I was unlocking the car
I was running for the bus
I was pushing a trolley round the supermarket
I was looking in a shop-window
I was cooking lunch
I was putting a cake in the oven
I was turning a sharp corner
I was watching the news

Ends
I fell off my bicycle
Somebody stole my purse
The phone went dead
I dropped the keys down a drain
My hat blew off
I knocked down a stack of tins
The dog knocked over the bucket of water
The television broke down
The electricity went off
I burnt my arm

21 **ask** (BEU 53)

ask or *ask for*? Put in *for* where necessary.

1 The policeman asked me _____ my name and address.
2 I asked her _____ the salt, but she didn't hear me.
3 If you get lost, ask a policeman _____ the way.
4 I felt ill, so I asked _____ to be excused.
5 I asked _____ the flowers to be delivered to my mother's address.
6 You shouldn't ask people _____ money.
7 He asked me _____ the time, but my watch had stopped.
8 Don't forget to ask him _____ the books he promised you.
9 I asked him _____ to lend me ten pounds, but he couldn't.
10 Don't forget to ask _____ the price of that house.

22 at, in and on (place) (BEU 54)

Look at this list, and write down the places where you
would expect to see these signs.
Answer with *at*, *in* or *on*, as in the example.

aeroplane	customs	shop
airport	garden gate	train
ambulance	Mercedes car	woollen
box	museum	clothing
cinema	park (twice)	zoo

► **on** leather goods

1	2	3	4
	GOODS to declare / NOTHING to declare		
5 Arrivals ↑ Transfers ↑	**6**	**7**	**8** FRAGILE
9 EMERGENCY EXIT	**10** Beware of the Dog	**11** Keep off the grass	**12** PLEASE DO NOT TOUCH
13 Please do not feed the animals	**14** DO NOT LEAN OUT OF THE WINDOW	**15** Please check your change	**16**

---

23 at, in and on (place) (BEU 54)

Where do you usually do some of the following things?
Use *at*, *in* or *on* and *a/the*.

► read the newspaper?
at home, **on** the bus, **in** the kitchen, etc

1 read the newspaper?
2 shop for food?
3 keep your bicycle/car?
4 post letters?
5 watch television?

6 go dancing?
7 buy records and cassettes?
8 wash your hair?
9 wait for the bus?
10 meet your friends?

---

24 at, in and on (time) (BEU 55)

When do you usually do some of the following things?
Begin with *at*, *in* or *on*.

► go swimming?
in summer, **at** weekends, **on** Saturdays, etc

1 go swimming?
2 read the newspaper?
3 go to bed?
4 see friends?
5 have parties?
6 have lunch?

7 receive presents?
8 visit relatives?
9 go shopping?
10 have a bath?
11 have breakfast?
12 go on holiday?

25 be + infinitive (BEU 58)

Put in the correct form of *be to*.

▶ The Queen *was to* visit New Zealand in autumn, but the trip was postponed.

1 You children _____ finish your homework before you watch television.
2 Our department _____ be moved to Edinburgh, but plans were changed at the last minute.
3 The Pope _____ visit Australia next year.
4 All competition entries _____ be submitted before 30th September.
5 The teacher said the children _____ be quiet until she came back.
6 I _____ be promoted to head of department within six months!
7 The staff _____ receive a 5 per cent rise, but they only got 3 per cent.
8 The medicine _____ be taken before meals.
9 All applicants for the job _____ be interviewed in May.
10 The examination _____ be held in May, but the date was changed to 15th June.

26 because and because of (BEU 60)

Which would you choose and why? Give as many reasons as you can.

▶ A holiday in Greece or a holiday in England?
I would choose a holiday in Greece because of the good weather.
I would choose a holiday in Greece because it is warmer there.
I would choose a holiday in England because of the language.
I would choose a holiday in England because I like speaking English.

1 A sports car or a saloon car?
2 Spaghetti and ice-cream for lunch or fruit and yoghurt?
3 A seaside holiday or a skiing holiday?
4 A big old house or a small modern house?
5 A house in the country or a flat in the city?
6 A job in your own country or a job abroad?

27 before (conjunction) (BEU 62)

What do you usually do first?

▶ clean your teeth, comb your hair?
I usually clean my teeth before I comb my hair.

1 have a shower, clean your teeth?
2 get dressed, comb your hair?
3 have breakfast, get dressed?
4 shave/put on your make-up, comb your hair?
5 put on your shoes, have breakfast?
6 have breakfast, make your bed?
7 read the newspaper, have lunch?
8 watch television, read the newspaper?
9 have supper, watch television?
10 get into bed, put out the light?

28 before (preposition) and in front of (BEU 63)

before or *in front of*?

1 I must go to the hairdresser's _____ the end of the week.
2 I've parked the car _____ the police station.
3 I couldn't see much at the theatre. There was a big fat man sitting right _____ me.
4 I arrived at the office just _____ nine.
5 I'll phone you _____ Wednesday.
6 Do you know the man who's standing _____ you?
7 We couldn't go faster. There was a lorry _____ us.
8 I've got so many things to do _____ the holidays.
9 We can't stop here. We're right _____ a 'No parking' sign.
10 Can you ring me _____ the concert?

big, large, great and tall (BEU 65)

How would you describe the following?
Use *big*, *large*, *great* or *tall* and a
suitable noun where necessary.

▶ Winston Churchill?
  *a **great** politician/man*

  a house with twelve rooms?
  *a **big/large** house*

1 Abraham Lincoln?
2 a 6-seater car?
3 a building with 30 storeys?
4 a mistake that you regretted?
5 a very good friend?

6 the USSR?
7 a very good idea?
8 a tree 30 metres high?
9 Ludwig van Beethoven?
10 a flat with six rooms?

30 borrow and lend (BEU 67)

Put in the correct form of *borrow* or *lend*.

1 Can you _____ me ten pounds until the
  weekend, please?
2 I'd like to _____ Mr Andrews' camera, but I don't
  suppose he'll want to _____ it to me.
3 Don't _____ money to Peggy! She always
  forgets to pay you back.
4 Why don't you _____ Jack's bicycle? I'm sure
  he wouldn't mind.
5 Susan Webber has _____ me her tennis racket.
  Hers is better than mine.

6 Dad, can I _____ your car for the evening?
7 _____ me your pen, will you? Mine won't write.
8 I don't like _____ things from my neighbours.
9 I can't _____ you my dictionary; I've already
  _____ it to Pamela.
10 I have a lot of figures to add up. I'll _____
  Jeremy's calculator.

31 both with verbs (BEU 69)

Compare the two brothers, using *both*.

▶ *They **both** like music.*
  *They can **both** swim.*

Continue . . .

	Jeff	Bill
likes music	×	×
can swim	×	×
is over 18	×	×
likes discos	×	
has been abroad	×	×
still goes to school		×
plays a musical instrument	×	×
hates examinations	×	×
enjoys mathematics	×	×
wants to become a doctor		×
likes dancing	×	×
can drive a car	×	×
speaks a foreign language	×	×
has a girlfriend	×	×
dislikes parties		×
can play chess	×	×

32 **bring** and **take** (BEU 71)

Put in the correct form of *bring* or *take*.

1 I've got a lot of money in my bag. I must _____ it to the bank immediately.
2 Could you _____ these letters to the post office for me?
3 John's very thoughtful. Whenever he comes, he always _____ flowers.
4 You mustn't forget to _____ these books back to the library.
5 If we go by car, we can _____ the dog with us.
6 Colin's going to _____ his new car round to show us.

7 You can _____ my dictionary home with you if you like, but please don't forget to _____ it back tomorrow.
8 Mrs Lewis said she would _____ the books to the office for me.
9 Oh dear. I forgot to _____ the car to the garage.
10 When you drive to Bristol, will you _____ me with you?

33 **can** and **could**: ability (BEU 78.1)

How well can you do these things? *Very well? Quite well? A bit? Not at all?*

► *I can swim **quite well**.*
   *I can't speak French **at all**.*

type	use a sewing machine	cook
drive a car	dance	dive
use a pocket calculator	paint	ride a bicycle
take photographs	act	play the guitar
play table tennis	play football	speak Japanese

Say how well you can do some other things.

34 **can**: ability (BEU 78.2)

What do you think people will be able to do two hundred years from now?
Begin: *I think/don't think people/we will be able to* . . .

1 live on another planet?
2 live in space?
3 live in towns on the sea-bed?
4 build cities in the desert?
5 go on holiday to the moon?
6 fly private helicopters and small planes?

7 grow food on the sea-bed?
8 travel faster than light?

Write some other things that you think/don't think people will be able to do in two hundred years.

35 **could**: ability (BEU 78.3)

Make some sentences with *could* and *couldn't*, as in the example.

► *I **could** speak my own language when I was four, but I **couldn't** speak English until I was 25/started this school/etc.*

Ideas:
speak your own language/speak English
walk/talk
count to ten/do geometry
say the alphabet/read
write your name/write a letter
swim/dive
play football/play chess
boil an egg/cook a meal
ride a bicycle/drive

an: possibility (BEU 79)

How long can they live? One number in each pair shows the average life span of the animals in years. Do you know which number is correct? If not, guess! Write a sentence like this:

▶ 12 or 20 years
*I think a tiger **can live** up to 20 years.* (Correct)

12 or 20 years

15 or 20 years

6 or 10 years

20 or 25 years

2 or 5 years

20 or 40 years

17 or 25 years

40 or 100 years

12 or 18 years

50 or 70 years

24 or 34 years

37 can: possibility (BEU 79.1)

> He's tall and slim, wearing a dark suit, dark hat and dark tie, carrying a black briefcase. He's about 35, has short dark hair and is clean-shaven without glasses.

This is a witness's description of a bank robber. Look carefully at the police suspects. Can the robber be one of them? Work it out like this:

▶ **It can't be** X because he's over 35/too small/has got a beard, etc.

38 could have: probability (BEU 79.3)

You have a friend who's very careless, but lucky. Nothing serious happened in the following situations, but what could have happened?

▶ She left her luggage unattended on a platform. *Someone **could have** stolen it.*

1 She left the house and forgot to close the kitchen window.
2 She left her purse in a shop.
3 She left the house and forgot to turn off the iron.
4 She drove the car after taking four sleeping pills.
5 She left her umbrella in a restaurant.

6 She wore high heeled shoes on the icy pavement.
7 She ran outside without a coat on a very cold day.
8 She jumped into a lake although she couldn't swim.
9 She climbed up a high tree to rescue a cat.
10 She parked her car in a no-parking zone.

39 **can**: permission, offers (BEU 80.1,3)

Asking permission. What do you think they are saying?
Use *can*.

1

2

3

4

Making offers. What do you think they are saying?
Use *can*.

5

6

7

8

40 could/couldn't: past permission (BEU 80.2)

When Joan was a student, she had a room in London.
The landlady was very strict. She put this notice on
Joan's door. What could/couldn't she do?

▶ Joan **couldn't** have visitors after 10 pm or on Sundays.
   She **could** only make drinks in the kitchen.

Continue . . .

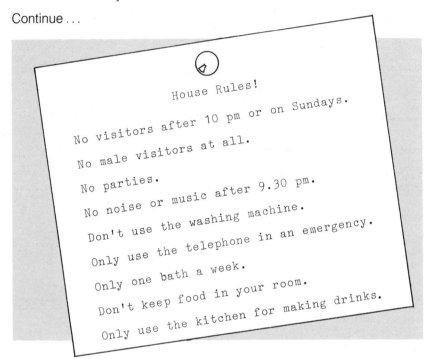

House Rules!

No visitors after 10 pm or on Sundays.

No male visitors at all.

No parties.

No noise or music after 9.30 pm.

Don't use the washing machine.

Only use the telephone in an emergency.

Only one bath a week.

Don't keep food in your room.

Only use the kitchen for making drinks.

Then write about some things that you *could/couldn't* do when you were younger.

---

41 come and go (BEU 83)

Put in the correct form of *come* or *go*.

1 Peter often _____ to visit us. We like him to _____,
  but he never knows when to _____ home!
2 Shall we _____ and see Janet next weekend?
  She _____ back from Edinburgh yesterday.
3 What time did you _____ to the doctor's
  yesterday?
4 'Will you _____ here, please? I want to show you
  something.' 'Okay. I'll _____ as soon as I can.'
5 'Can I _____ and visit you tomorrow?' 'Of
  course! You're welcome to _____ any time!'
6 We _____ to Brighton yesterday. It was lovely!
7 We _____ to live in Manchester in 1965 and
  we've felt very happy here.
8 Tim's five. He _____ to school now.
9 I'm _____ into hospital soon. Will you _____
  and visit me?

---

42 comparison: comparative adjectives (BEU 84)

Compare yourself and your best friend.
Use comparatives of *fat, thin, dark, fair, tall, small,
young, old, cheerful, clever, intelligent, practical,
polite, musical, strong, happy*.

▶ I'm **fatter** than he/she is.
   He's/She's **more intelligent** than I am.

43 comparison: superlative adjectives (BEU 84)

Compare the hotels using superlatives of *big, cheap, expensive, far, luxurious, modern, near, new, old, small.*

▶ *The Palm Beach is the **biggest**.*

Hotel Atlantis ★★★★★	**Hotel Astoria** ★★★	**Hotel Palm Beach** ★★★★
● Built 1978	● Built 1970	● Built 1982
● 350 rooms	● 100 rooms	● 400 rooms
● 500m to beach	● 700m to beach	● 200m to beach
● 400m to centre	● 300m to centre	● 800m to centre
● 1 week from £334	● 1 week from £205	● 1 week from £260

44 comparison: superlative adjectives (BEU 85.5)

▶ *The Queen Elizabeth II can carry 1,800 passengers. It's the **largest** passenger ship in the world.*

Now make similar statements about the following. Use superlatives of *big, busy, cold, dry, fast, high, large, long, tall, wet.*

1 Egypt has only 55.8 mm of rain a year.
2 Concorde flies at a speed of approximately 2,150 k/h.
3 The Toronto Tower is 553 m tall.
4 The River Nile is 6,678 km long.
5 Antarctica has an average temperature of −60°C.
6 The Sahara Desert covers an area of 8,400,000 sq km.
7 Mount Everest is 8,848 m high.
8 Mexico City has a population of about 17 million people.
9 Colombia has as much as 4,099 mm of rain a year.
10 At Chicago International Airport a plane takes off or lands every 45 seconds.

45 comparison: **much**, **far** etc with comparatives (BEU 86)

This is a list of world temperatures on 1 September 1984. Compare the temperatures using *a lot, a little, no, very much* and *warmer, cooler, hotter, colder,* as appropriate.

▶ Las Palmas/Tenerife
*It was **a little cooler** in Las Palmas than in Tenerife.*
Edinburgh/London
*It was (**very**) **much colder** in Edinburgh than in London.*
Cairo/Edinburgh
*It was **far hotter** in Cairo than in Edinburgh.*

	WORLD TEMPERATURES Lunch time reports				
	°C	°F		°C	°F
Alexandria	28	82	Madrid	27	80
Barcelona	25	77	Malaga	20	68
Cairo	30	86	Melbourne	16	60
Edinburgh	12	53	Moscow	12	53
Glasgow	14	57	Munich	30	86
Helsinki	13	55	Riyadh	39	102
Las Palmas	28	82	Stockholm	23	73
London	20	68	Sydney	23	73
Luxor	35	100	Tenerife	30	86

1 Alexandria/Cairo
2 Glasgow/Edinburgh
3 Malaga/London
4 Helsinki/Stockholm
5 Riyadh/Alexandria
6 Cairo/Munich
7 Edinburgh/Moscow
8 Luxor/Alexandria
9 Barcelona/Madrid
10 Melbourne/Sydney

46 conditional: progressive conditional (BEU 88.1)

What would they be doing if . . . ?

▶ He's doing his homework.
If he wasn't doing his homework,
he'd be playing *football.* (1)

1 He's doing his homework.

2 He's teaching.

3 He's having a hard day at the office.

4 She's working late.

5 He's mending his car.

6 She's doing the housework.

7 He's practising the piano.

---

47 conditional: use (BEU 88.2a)

What would you do if. . . ?

▶ Suppose someone stole your car. . .
If someone stole my car I **would** *report it to the police immediately.*

1 Suppose you left a restaurant with the wrong umbrella. . .
2 Suppose a waiter in a restaurant overcharged you. . .
3 Suppose you missed the last bus home. . .
4 Suppose you missed your station on the train. . .
5 Suppose you got lost in a big city. . .

6 Suppose someone stole your wallet. . .
7 Suppose you lost your passport. . .
8 Suppose a stranger asked you for a lift at night. . .
9 Suppose someone offered you a briefcase full of money. . .
10 Suppose you got stuck in a lift. . .

conjunctions (BEU 89.3)

Say these things another way. Use *because*, *so*, *although*, *but*, *as*, *that*.

▶ Because I hadn't worked hard enough, I didn't pass the exam.
   *I hadn't worked hard enough, **so** I didn't pass the exam.*

1 As we all know, English is a difficult language to learn well.
2 You can see that I'm very busy.
3 Although the sun's shining, it isn't very warm.
4 He's very rich, but he doesn't waste money.
5 I hadn't saved enough money, so I couldn't buy a car.
6 Because I liked him, I trusted him.
7 I didn't trust him, so I didn't help him.
8 As you will understand, I can't pay the whole sum at once.
9 She's very busy, but she's always willing to help.
10 Although he's very fat, he doesn't eat much.

---

49 'copula' verbs (BEU 91)

Describe these pictures with *look*, *sound*, *smell*, *taste* or *feel*, as in the example. Use *beautiful*, *bitter*, *burnt*, *delicious*, *delightful*, *expensive*, *hot*, *lonely*, *soft*, *cold*, *sad*, *happy*, *terrible*.

▶ *They **look** happy.*   (1)

1

2

3

4

5

6

7

8

9

10

11

12

13

50 countable and uncountable nouns (BEU 92)

Use *a/an* or no article, as necessary.

▶ *English people often have:*
orange juice, cornflakes (or other cereal),
porridge, boiled eggs, bacon (or ham) and eggs,
toast or rolls with butter, jam or marmalade, tea or
coffee.

Simon has:
*a glass of orange juice, **a** boiled egg, **a** piece of*
toast with butter and jam, two cups of tea.

1 What do people in your country often have for breakfast?
2 What do you usually have for breakfast?

51 dates (BEU 95)

Can you match the horoscope
signs with the dates? Say the dates
aloud and write them in words
(either British English or American
English).

▶ *Aquarius, from January the*
twenty-first to February the
nineteenth. (British English)

21st January – 19th February
20th February – 20th March
21st March – 20th April
21st April – 21st May
22nd May – 21st June
22nd June – 23rd July
24th July – 23rd August
24th August – 23rd September
24th September – 23rd October
24th October – 22nd November
23rd November – 21st December
22nd December – 20th January

52 dates (BEU 95.2)

When and where did the Olympic Games take place?
Say the date aloud and write it in words.

▶ 1960, Rome or Athens?
In 1960 (nineteen sixty), the Olympic Games were held in Rome.

1 1964, Tokyo or Madrid?
2 1968, Lisbon or Mexico City?
3 1972, Delhi or Munich?

4 1976, Montreal or Buenos Aires?
5 1980, Budapest or Moscow?
6 1984, London or Los Angeles?

53 **do**: auxiliary verb (BEU 98.1,2)

Which of these things don't you do?
Which of these things can't you do?

▶ I **don't** listen to jazz.
   I **can't** write shorthand.

drink strong coffee	like snakes
stay out late at night	travel a lot
go to bed early	enjoy walking
smoke	ski
believe in horoscopes	like horror films
like music	listen to jazz
write shorthand	play the trumpet
speak Chinese	watch much television
drive a car	enjoy washing up

54 **do + -ing** (BEU 99)

Make 10 true sentences.

▶ I don't **do** much **cleaning** at the weekends.

I	do don't do	a lot of much some the my	shopping cleaning swimming etc	at the weekends in the evenings in winter etc.

55 **do** and **make** (BEU 100)

Continue the two columns, as in the example.

do...	make...
homework	a mistake

a mistake, homework, a favour, a journey, the beds, a cake, housework, bread, arrangements, a decision, business, the washing-up, an excuse, one's best, one's duty, the shopping, a model plane, a phone call, the cooking, military service

56 **during** and **for** (BEU 101)

during or for?

CAROL   I'm going to Mexico __1__ two months this summer.

PAT   Oh, it's a fascinating country. I was there __2__ the summer vacation last year, but only __3__ a month. I'm going to India this year.

CAROL   I stayed in Calcutta __4__ a while a few years ago. I met some very interesting people there __5__ my stay. I went to Canada last year with two friends, on a peaceful fishing holiday. It was certainly peaceful – we didn't see anyone else __6__ three weeks! __7__ the day it was beautiful, but __8__ the night we often heard strange noises and couldn't get to sleep __9__ hours. In summer it's lovely and warm, but I wouldn't like to be there __10__ the winter.

63 enough (BEU 113.2)

Ted's going to have a party. He needs more food and drink etc. Look at his list. Say what he has got/hasn't got enough of.

▶ *He's got **enough** orange juice.*

	need	have got
orange juice	4 bottles	4 bottles
Coca Cola	4 bottles	1 bottle
beer	6 bottles	2 bottles
wine	2 bottles	2 bottles
sausage rolls	12	3
cheese biscuits	3 packets	1 packet
packets of crisps	4 packets	4 packets
chocolate biscuits	3 packets	4 packets
glasses	6	5
plates	6	6
chairs	6	2

64 enough (BEU 113.3)

In your country, is a young person of 16 old enough to do these things?
▶ vote?
*He/she isn't **old enough** to vote.*

1 vote?
2 ride a motor-bike?
3 leave school?
4 buy cigarettes?
5 drive a car?
6 open a bank account?
7 earn money?
8 live alone?
9 be sent to prison?
10 get married?

65 even though (BEU 114.4)

Rewrite with *Even though*, as in the example.

▶ Mary's very pretty, but she hasn't got a boyfriend.
Even though *Mary's very pretty, she hasn't got a boyfriend.*

1 I didn't work very hard for the exam, but I passed.
2 I don't speak Greek, but I made a lot of friends in Athens.
3 Mr Collins doesn't earn much, but he's always well dressed.
4 Sylvia hasn't got many friends, but she's always out.
5 Robert hasn't had a good education, but he's got a good job.
6 Jill Stewart has four children, but her house is always clean and tidy.
7 Mrs Poole doesn't eat much, but she puts on weight.
8 Terry has stopped smoking, but he still has a cough.
9 The sun didn't shine all day, but it was very warm.
10 I sat in the shade all day, but I got a sun-tan.

66 ever (BEU 116)

You would like to know more about a person who interests you. Ask him/her questions with *Have you ever...? Do you ever...?* Think of your own interests and the places you have been to.

▶ ***Do you ever*** *go to discos?*
Have you ever *been to America?*

67 **except** and **except for** (BEU 119)

Which one is different? Make sentences with *all* and
except, as in the example.

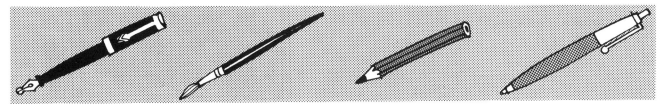

► *They're **all** used for writing (We write with them all/They all write) **except** the paintbrush.*
or
*They **all** have metal parts **except** the pencil.*

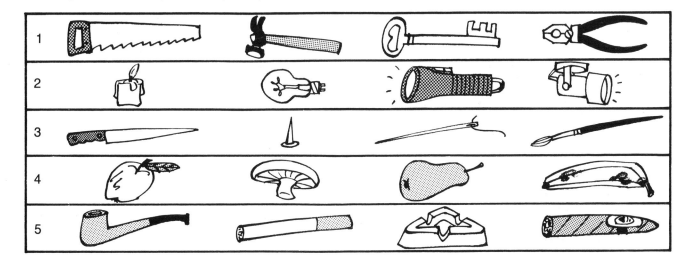

Now make sentences with *except for* and *all*, as in the example.

► ***Except for** the tyre, they are **all** completely round.*

79 **for** + object + infinitive (BEU (132.1)

Answer these questions about your country as in the example.

> Do women go out to work? *(common/unusual)*
> Yes, it's common **for women to go out to work**.
> No, it's unusual **for women to go out to work**.

1 Do pupils attend school until they are 16 or older? *(usual/rare)*
2 Do people own a house or flat? *(common/rare)*
3 Do people have several children? *(normal/uncommon)*
4 Do women usually have a driving licence? *(common/rare)*
5 Do old people live with their children? *(usual/uncommon)*

6 Do women join the armed forces? *(common/rare)*
7 Do unmarried couples live together? *(common/unusual)*
8 Do people usually join a political party or trade union? *(usual/rare)*
9 Are great numbers of people unemployed? *(common/rare)*
10 Do people learn English at school? *(normal/unusual)*

---

80 **for** + object + infinitive (BEU 132.1)

Rewrite as in the example.

> ▶ People in Britain often fail their driving test the first time. *(It's normal...)*
> It's normal **for people in Britain to fail** their driving test the first time.

1 Learners often have to take their driving test three times. *(It's also quite common...)*
2 Most people pass the test the second time. *(It's usual...)*
3 All beginners should take some lessons with a driving instructor. *(It's important...)*
4 The driving instructor usually points out mistakes. *(It's usual...)*
5 Learner drivers should keep their eyes on the road, not on the signs. *(It's essential...)*

6 Nervous drivers should try to keep calm. *(It's important...)*
7 The learner should try to feel confident and not panic. *(It's quite essential...)*
8 Most people usually feel very nervous on the day of the test. *(It's quite normal...)*
9 Examiners are usually quite strict. *(It's usual...)*
10 A nervous driver doesn't usually pass the test the first time. *(It's rare...)*

---

81 **for** and **since** (BEU 133.1–3)

This is Bill   and this is Mary.

Here are some facts about them. Put in *for* (6 times) and *since* (4 times) with the date (year) or number of years, as in the example.

Bill was born in 1950. He met Mary when he was 20. Now he's 35, so he's known her *for 15 years*. They got married 12 years ago, when Bill was 23. Now it's 1985, so they've been married ___1___ . Bill started work when he was 18, so he had worked ___2___ before he got married. After they got married in 1973, Mary kept her job until 1979, so she worked ___3___ after their marriage. Then they had a child. Now he's 6. Bill has worked for his present firm for 10 years, ___4___ . He's an accountant. Before then, he worked for a smaller firm. He started there in 1971, so altogether he worked for them ___5___ . Bill and Mary bought a house 5 years ago, so they've had it ___6___ . They bought a new car 2 years ago, so they've had that ___7___ . Their last holiday was in 1982 – no money, so they haven't been on holiday ___8___ . Their little boy started school at the age of 5, so he's been going to school ___9___ . Three months later, Mary started a part-time job, so she's had the job ___10___ .

82 **for** and **since**   (BEU 133.4)

How long have you been doing these things?
Answer with *for* or *since* the questions that apply to you.

▶ How long have you been learning English?
   *I've been learning English **for three years**/**since 1982**.*

1 How long have you lived in your town?
2 How long have your parents lived in your town?
3 How long have you been living in your present house/flat?
4 How long have you been able to ride a bicycle/ drive a car?

5 How long have you had a bicycle/car?
6 How long have you known your best friend?
7 How long have you known your English teacher?
8 How long have you been able to swim?
9 How long have you been engaged/married?
10 How long have you had your present job?

83 future: present progressive   (BEU 135.1)

Say what you are doing (or what somebody else is doing) at the following times.

▶ after supper tonight?
   *I'm **going straight to bed** after supper tonight.*

   tomorrow evening?
   *My sister's **going out** tomorrow evening.*

1 After supper tonight?
2 Tomorrow evening?
3 On Saturday?
4 On Sunday?
5 On your/his/her next holiday?

84 future: **going to**   (BEU 135.2)

What's going to happen?

▶ *The car's **going to** overturn.*   (1)

1

2

7

6

3

4

5

6

8

9

85 future: **going to** (BEU 135.2)

What are you going to do this evening? Are you going
to do any of the following things?

▶   I'm **going to watch** television.
     I'm not **going to wash** my hair.

86 future: **shall**/**will** (predictions) (BEU 136)

What will life be like 100 years from now? Here are some ideas:

▶ *There won't be any more cars. Most people will fly private helicopters. Robots will do housework. Computers will do office work. Children won't have to go to school; they'll learn from computers at home.*

> **Ideas**
>
> | computers | leisure time |
> |---|---|
> | space travel | travel |
> | traffic | air pollution |
> | cars | supersonic planes |
> | working conditions | population explosion |
> | robots | |

87 future: **shall**/**will** (predictions) (BEU 136)

What questions would you ask a fortune-teller?
Begin with *Will . . .* and *What/When/How long/Where* etc.

▶ *Will I get married?*
What will my husband/wife be like?
Where will I live?

88 future: simple present (BEU 138.1)

What are Jim's travel arrangements for his trip to the International Book Fair in Frankfurt?
Use *depart, arrive, cross, stay, travel,* etc.

▶ *He **leaves** Doncaster by train at 16.10 and . . .*

```
dep. Doncaster 16.10
arr. London, Kings Cross 17.49
overnight in London, Victoria Hotel
dep. London, Victoria 8.00
arr. Dover 9.25
Jetfoil 10.00
arr. Ostend 11.40
dep. Ostend 12.15
arr. Frankfurt 19.10
```

89 future perfect (BEU 139)

The table shows the most densely populated cities/areas of the world in millions, with approximate estimates for the year 2000.

Compare the information as in the examples:

▶ *By the year 2000, the population of Mexico will have increased from 15 million to 26.3 million.*

By the year 2000, Mexico will have moved up to first position.

By the year 2000, New York will have gone down to sixth position.

	1980	m		2000	m
1	Tokyo	17.0	1	Mexico City	26.3
2	New York	15.6	2	São Paulo	24.0
3	Mexico City	13.0	3	Tokyo	17.1
4	São Paulo	12.8	4	Calcutta	16.6
5	Shanghai	11.8	5	Bombay	16.0
6	Buenos Aires	10.1	6	New York	15.5
7	London	10.0	7	Seoul	13.5
8	Calcutta	9.5	8	Shanghai	13.5
9	Los Angeles	9.5	9	Rio de Janeiro	13.3
10	Rhine-Ruhr (W. Germany)	9.3	10	Delhi	13.3
11	Rio de Janeiro	9.2	11	Buenos Aires	13.2
12	Beijing	9.1	12	Cairo	13.2

Write about Tokyo São Paulo Shanghai Buenos Aires Calcutta Rio de Janeiro Bombay Seoul

90 future perfect (BEU 139)

How much will they have saved? Write sentences.

▶ *Terry will have saved £100 in 2 months' time.*

1	Terry, in 3 months' time?	
2	Janet, in 6 weeks' time?	
3	Ted, in 4 months' time?	
4	Maria, in 6 months' time?	
5	Barry, in a month's time?	
6	Jeff, in 10 weeks' time?	
7	Helen, in 3 months' time?	
8	Celia, in a month's time?	
9	Betty, in 10 weeks' time?	
10	John, in 10 weeks' time?	

Terry	£50 a month
Janet	£8 a week
Ted	£65 a month
Maria	£100 a month
Barry	spends everything
Jeff	£6 a week
Helen	£70 a month
Celia	doesn't save
Betty	£10 a week
John	spends everything

How much will you have saved six months from now?

---

91 future progressive (BEU 140)

Mr Green is flying to Paris tomorrow. Here's his notebook.

What will he be doing tomorrow at the following times?

▶ 6.20
At 6.20 tomorrow he'll be driving to the airport by taxi.

1	8.00	5	10.15	9	15.45
2	8.55	6	12.15	10	16.30
3	9.20	7	14.15	11	18.00
4	9.30	8	15.00	12	18.30

6·15 taxi to airport
7·30 flight leaves
8·55 arrival / Paris
9·20 meet M. Chevalier, drive to company headquarters
10·00 meeting with Board of Directors
12·00 lunch with Max Peters
14·00 lecture (don't forget lecture notes!)
15·00 phone New York !
15·30 meeting with Bill Morris (project CX12)
16·30 leave for airport
17·00 arrival at airport
18·00 flight home leaves
19·30 flight lands

---

92 get + noun/pronoun, adjective (BEU 142.1,2)

What does *get* mean in the following sentences?

1 The phone's ringing. I'll *get* it.
2 I was in the supermarket today, so I *got* you some of those cheap chocolate biscuits.
3 We couldn't go to London because Fred *got* flu.
4 I can't *get* the lid off the jar of jam.
5 What time did you *get* there?
6 Can you *get* Luxemburg on your transistor?
7 I'm sorry, but I didn't *get* the joke.
8 You didn't *get* the thief, but did you at least *get* the car number?
9 Hurry up and eat your breakfast, before it *gets* cold!
10 How did you *get* the piano through the door?
11 The shop had sold out of those new tin openers, but they're going to *get* me one.
12 I *got* a parcel from Aunt Susan this morning.

93 go: been and gone (BEU 145.1)

Where has he been? Write sentences saying
which cities/countries Mr Smith has been to.

▶ **He's been** to Athens/Greece. (1)

Which foreign countries have you been to?
Think of people you know who are abroad at the moment.
Say where they have *gone*.

▶ *My father's **gone** to Mexico.*

99 **have (got)**: possession etc (BEU 153.2)

Have you or your family got any of these?

▶   I'**ve got** a tent.
   We **haven't got** a piano.
   My brother'**s got** a bicycle.

100 **have**: actions (BEU 154)

Say what Frank and Janet do and
when they do it. Use *have*.

▶ Before breakfast
*Frank **has a shower**
before breakfast.*

Before breakfast

At 8 o'clock

At 10 o'clock

At 12.30

After lunch

At 3 o'clock

After work

In the evening: sometimes

In the evening: usually

At the weekend: often

At the weekend: sometimes

101 **have** + object + past participle (BEU 155.2)

What are they having done?

► *She's **having her**
  hair done. (1)

1

2

3

4

5

6

7

8

9

10

11

102 **have** + object + past participle (BEU 155.2)

Have you ever had any of these things done?

▶ your eyes tested?
*No, I've never **had my eyes tested**.*
*Yes, I've **had my eyes tested** twice/several times.*

1 a tooth extracted?
2 your heart examined?
3 your hearing tested?
4 your blood pressure checked?
5 a blood sample taken?
6 your lungs X-rayed?

103 **have (got) to** (BEU 156)

What have you got to do? Write ten sentences about things that you've got to do next week.

▶ *On Monday, I'**ve got to go** to the dentist's.*

104 **have (got) to** (BEU 156)

What do you think are the disadvantages of these jobs? Use *you have to...*

▶ air hostess
You **have to travel** most of the time. You **have to work** irregular hours. You **have to deal with** difficult passengers.

1 businessman
2 coal miner
3 factory worker
4 football player
5 hairdresser
6 photographic model
7 office worker
8 postman
9 shop assistant
10 waitress

105 **hear** and **listen (to)** (BEU 157)

Put in a form of *hear, listen* or *listen to*.

POLICEMAN Now, what exactly did you __1__ on the night of the murder?
MRS GREEN Well, I could __2__ loud voices next door – a man and a woman, but I was busy in the kitchen, so I wasn't really __3__ what they were saying. But then I __4__ a loud bang! So I stopped what I was doing to __5__ .
POLICEMAN What was your husband doing at the time?
MRS GREEN Well, he was __6__ a music programme on the radio. I told him to turn it down so that I could __7__ better. But he's rather deaf, so he didn't __8__ me. And he never really __9__ what I say, in any case. But then the shouting started. I put my ear to the wall and __10__ as well as I could. I

__11__ the man say quite clearly: 'You'll never cheat me again!' And then the shots! I couldn't believe it!
POLICEMAN Did your husband __12__ the shots as well?
MRS GREEN No, the music was too loud, and he says he wasn't __13__ anyway.

106 home (BEU 161)

Complete with a suitable verb + *home*. Use each verb once: *arrive, bring, come, drive, get, go, leave, reach, run, take, walk*.

▶ *We left early in the morning, but we didn't* **reach home** *until late evening.*

1 We _____ at 8 am and arrived in Edinburgh at 4 pm.
2 It's very late. I really must _____ now.
3 Goodbye! Have a good time and don't _____ late!
4 If you leave now, you should _____ at about 6 o'clock.
5 We'll pack for the weekend, but if we don't find a hotel room, we'll simply _____ .

6 My wife's picking blackberries in the woods. Last Sunday she _____ nearly four pounds.
7 What time did you _____ last night?
8 There was a thunderstorm on the way, so we _____ as fast as we could.
9 I missed the last bus, so I had to _____ .
10 Bill doesn't earn much money. He says he _____ only a hundred pounds a week.

107 if: ordinary tenses (BEU 164.1)

What happens if . . . ? Complete the sentences.

▶ If you don't get enough sleep, *you always feel tired.*
If you sit in the hot sun for too long, you get sunburnt.

1 If you stand in the cold for a long time, _____ .
2 If you run uphill, _____ .
3 If you drink too much alcohol, _____ .
4 If you get caught in the rain without an umbrella, _____ .
5 If you don't have a job, _____ .

6 _____ , you put on weight.
7 _____ , you lose weight.
8 _____ , your eyes get tired.
9 _____ , you get a smoker's cough.
10 _____ , you get tooth decay.

108 if: special tenses (BEU 165.1)

What would you do/buy etc if you won the following amounts of money in your own currency?

1 £10   3 £1,000   5 £100,000
2 £100   4 £10,000   6 £1,000,000

109 **if**: special tenses, present and future situations (BEU 165.1)

If you hired the following models,
how much would it cost?

▶ a Vauxhall Astra for 3 days?
  If you **hired** *a Vauxhall Astra for
  3 days it* **would cost** *£66.00.*

1 a Ford Sierra for a weekend?
2 a BL Metro for 3 days?
3 a BMW 316 for 2 weeks?
4 a Ford Fiesta for 5 days?
5 a BL Montego for a week?
6 a Ford Orion for 2 weeks?
7 a Vauxhall Nova for a weekend?
8 a Ford Escort for 4 days?
9 a BL Maestro for 2 weeks?
10 a Vauxhall Cavalier for 3 weeks?

Hertz ®

LONDON BUDGET RATES
Pre-discounted rate. Must be pre-booked

GROUP	SEATS	Specific car models cannot be guaranteed MANUAL TRANSMISSION	SUNROOF	POWER STEERING	CASSETTE	RADIO	CARS MUST BE RETURNED TO RENTING BRANCH		
							DAILY UNLIMITED	WEEKLY UNLIMITED	WEEKEND ★ Fri 13·00hrs Mon 10·00hrs UNLIMITED
A	4	**FORD** Fiesta VAUXHALL Nova BL Metro				•	£20·50	£108·50	£42·00
B	4	**FORD** Escort 1.3L VAUXHALL Astra 1.3L BL Maestro 1.3L		•		•	£22·00	£119·00	£47·00
C	5	**FORD** Sierra 1.6L **FORD** Orion 1.6L VAUXHALL Cavalier 1.6L BL Montego 1.6L		•	•	•	£25·50	£140·00	£53·00
D	4	BMW 316	•		•	•	£38·50	£199·00	£85·00

---

110 **if**: special tenses, past situations (BEU 165.3)

You have a friend who is careless with his/her things.
Say what would/wouldn't have happened if he/she had/hadn't done the following:

▶ He left his suitcase unattended at an airport. It got stolen.
  If he **hadn't left** *his suitcase unattended, it* **wouldn't have got** *stolen.*

1 She forgot to lock the car. Her camera got stolen.
2 He left his wallet in a restaurant. It disappeared.
3 She left her watch lying about. It got broken.
4 He didn't lock the door of his flat. Thieves broke in.
5 She knocked her glasses off the table. They broke.
6 She didn't put her name on her suitcase. Someone took it by mistake.

7 He parked his car without lights. Another car ran into it.
8 He didn't look after his bicycle. It went rusty.
9 She left her parcels on a bus. Someone took them.
10 He didn't keep his passport in a safe place. It got lost.

---

111 **if**: special tenses, past situations (BEU 165.3)

Jim's holiday to Tangier cost more than necessary. It would have cost less if he had done some things differently.

Jim flew from Manchester in June and stayed at the Casino Park Hotel. He booked a single room with full board and a view of the sea.

▶ *It* **would have cost** *less if he* **hadn't booked** *a room with a view of the sea.*

Continue...

From Gatwick to Tangier:

SUN TRAVEL

	Palace	Casino Park	
Departure May	£185	£210	(7 nights)
Departure June	£220	£245	

From Manchester: + £40

Extra charges (per person per night)
full board £3   Single room £2
Room with view of the sea £1.50

112 **if**-sentences with **could** (BEU 166)

Your friend can't decide where to go on holiday. Make some suggestions about where he/she could go and what he/she could do. (He/She could visit famous buildings; practise languages; eat national dishes; do/watch certain sports.)

▶ Spain
*If you went to Spain, you **could** eat paella, lie in the sun, watch a bull-fight and speak Spanish.*

1	London	6	India
2	Scotland	7	Mexico
3	New York	8	Egypt
4	Paris	9	Switzerland
5	Kenya	10	Italy

113 **if only** (BEU 167)

Molly, Patsy, Richard and Frank all have regrets.

▶ Molly can't swim very well.
*She often thinks to herself, '**If only** I **could** swim well.*

Richard broke off his engagement.
*He often thinks to himself, '**If only** I **hadn't broken** off my engagement.'*

1 Patsy can't speak a foreign language.
2 Frank sold his old car.
3 Molly is afraid of water.
4 Richard failed his driving test.
5 Frank didn't take A-Level English at school.
6 Patsy left school at 16.
7 Molly can't play a musical instrument.
8 Richard didn't go to America when he had the chance.
9 Frank doesn't play tennis.
10 Richard isn't a good businessman.

114 imperative (BEU 170)

What advice would you give a friend who is going for a job interview? Here are some suggestions:

▶ ***Go to bed*** *early the night before.*
Don't be *nervous.*
Don't wear *your old jeans!*
Have *a good breakfast – and **eat** it all.*

Continue . . .

115 imperative (BEU 170.1)

The Green Cross code tells you how to cross a road safely. Put in: *cross, find, give, keep, let, listen, look* (2), *move, remember, run, stand* (2), *stop, try, walk* (2). Be careful, some need *don't*!

1 First, _____ a safe place to cross, then _____ .
_____ to cross between parked cars. _____ to a clear space and always _____ drivers a chance to see you clearly.
2 _____ on the pavement near the kerb.
_____ too near the edge of the pavement.
3 _____ all around for traffic and _____ .
You can sometimes hear traffic before you can see it.
4 If traffic is coming, _____ it pass. _____ all round again.

5 When there is no traffic, _____ straight across the road.
If there is something in the distance, _____ unless you are certain there's plenty of time.
_____ , even if traffic is a long way away, it may be coming very fast. When it's safe, _____ straight across – _____ !
6 _____ looking and listening for traffic while you cross.

116 imperative: with **do** (BEU 170.1)

Do you own a dog? The Dog Owners' Code tells you
how to look after a dog properly.
Complete it with *do* or *don't* + a suitable verb. Use
exercise, feed, have, keep (3), *leave, let* (3), *see.*

▶ *Do keep* him well under control in the country.

1 _____ him regularly. He needs a good run where it's safe.
2 _____ him run loose on the road.
3 _____ him clean – frequent brushing is the best way.
4 _____ him in a car with all the windows closed.
5 _____ that he has a dry place to sleep.
6 _____ children tease him.

7 _____ him regularly – one or two good meals every day at the same time. He needs fresh water too.
8 _____ him tied up or shut up for long periods.
9 _____ your name and address marked on his collar in case he gets lost.
10 _____ him foul pavements or grass areas.

117 **in case** (BEU 172.1,2)

Some friends are going on a day's hike. Tell them what
to take with them, just in case certain things happen.

▶ Take sleeping bags, **in case** you don't get home tonight.

1 Take warm pullovers _____ .
2 Take plenty to drink _____ .
3 Take enough food _____ .
4 Take waterproof clothing

   _____ .
5 Take a map _____ .
6 Take a compass _____ .

7 Take your sunglasses

   _____ .
8 Take some sticking plasters

   _____ .
9 Take some money _____ .
10 Take some kind of identification _____ .

118 **in spite of** (BEU 173)

You have a friend who's very headstrong and does
things in spite of advice and warnings. Rewrite the
sentences, with *in spite of* + noun.

▶ He bought an old car, although it was in a bad condition.
*He bought an old car **in spite of** its bad condition.*

1 He drove the car 200 kilometres, although the roads were icy.
2 He drove the car up narrow mountain roads, although it was dangerous.
3 He tried to repair the car himself, although he was inexperienced as a mechanic.
4 He drove the car at night, although it was foggy.
5 He went sailing in his boat, although the weather forecast was bad.
6 He walked 10 kilometres, although it was snowing heavily.
7 He went out in the cold, although he was ill.

8 He smoked forty cigarettes a day, although his doctor warned him to stop smoking.
9 He bought an old house, although the price was high.
10 He married a girl who didn't suit him, although I advised him not to.

119 infinitive: verb + object + infinitive (BEU 176.3)

What do these advertisements want people to do?

▶ *Number one **wants people to book** a cruise.*
*Number two **wants you to invest** money.*

Continue...

120   infinitive: verb + object + infinitive   (BEU 176.3)

Have you ever been swimming in Hawaii? If not, here's a warning to newcomers.

BEACH SAFETY

Hawaii's beaches are breathtakingly beautiful, but they can be very dangerous for newcomers. The beaches are always open, even when there is no lifeguard protection. If you do not see a lifeguard on duty, swim on another beach. Remember:

- Never turn your back on the ocean.
- Enter the water slowly and carefully.
- Don't be caught off your guard.
- Never swim alone.
- Always have someone you can call to.
- Dive beneath breaking waves before they reach you.
- Do not stand in the path of a large wave.
- Do not swim over a large wave or turn your back against it.
- Avoid beaches with rocky coasts.
- Stay clear of areas with surfers.
- Look out for runaway surfboards that wash in with the waves.

What does the warning *advise/remind/tell/warn* you to do or not to do?

▶   It **advises** you to swim on another beach if you don't see a lifeguard on duty.
    It **warns** you never to turn your back on the ocean.

Continue. . .

121   infinitive after **who**, **what**, **how** etc   (BEU 177.1)

A group of young Americans has come to stay in your town/area. What would you tell them/show them?
In your answers, use *who/when/where/what/whether/ how + (not) to.*

▶   I would tell them **where to eat**.
    I would show them **how to use** the buses.

Ideas:

hotels	shopping
transport	culture
sightseeing	money
entertainment	clothing
museums	information centres

122 infinitive of purpose (BEU 178)

Why would you go there?
Answer with *to. . .*

▶ *I'd go to a travel agency **to book** a holiday.* (1)

1

2

3

4

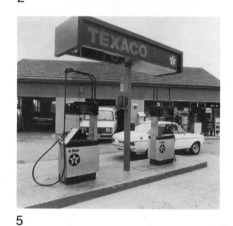

5

6

7

8

9

10

11

123 infinitive of purpose (BEU 178)

Why do some people need or use these things?

▶ sleeping pills
Some people need sleeping pills **to help** *them to sleep.*

1	an alarm clock	6	make-up
2	a walking stick	7	perfume/aftershave
3	glasses	8	artificial sweeteners
4	a hearing aid	9	medicine and tablets
5	hair dye	10	a safe

124 infinitive of purpose (BEU 178)

People all over the world learn English at evening classes or in special courses.
Why do you think the following groups of people need/want to learn English?
Use *in order to/so as to...*

▶ Hotel receptionists
Hotel receptionists need English **in order to** *talk to foreign guests.*

1	businessmen and -women	5	pilots
2	secretaries	6	housewives
3	scientists	7	journalists
4	engineers	8	people in the travel business

125 -ing form ('gerund') (BEU 180.2)

What are your hobbies? Name six things that you enjoy.

▶ *taking photographs, driving, listening to music,
playing chess, swimming, cooking.*

126 -ing form ('gerund') after verb: (BEU 180.3)

Study these activities:

going shopping	wasting time
standing in crowded buses	sunbathing
chatting on the telephone	cooking
borrowing money	sewing on buttons
looking after children	arguing about money
making excuses	making new friends
getting up early	waiting at the doctor's
watching horror films	doing examinations
writing thank-you letters	sleeping late
taking on responsibility	smoking
	repairing things

Name all the things that...

▶ ... you usually try to avoid
I usually try to avoid **standing** *in crowded buses.*

1 ... you usually try to avoid.
2 ... you dislike.
3 ... you enjoy.
4 ... you often feel like.
5 ... you would like to give up.
6 ... you don't mind.
7 ... you often try to put off.
8 ... you don't like to risk.
9 ... you can't stand.

127 -ing form ('gerund') after **need** and **want** (BEU 180.4)

What needs doing?

▶   *The bed **needs making**.*

---

128 -ing form ('gerund') after preposition (BEU 180.5)

How can you become a millionaire?
Think of as many quick ways as possible, using
by . . . ing, as in the example.

▶   ***By making** a successful pop record.*
***By robbing** a bank!*

129 -ing form or infinitive? (BEU 182.1)

A friend of yours is going on holiday. Remind him of the things he must do.

► lock the door
Remember to/Don't forget to lock the door.

1 close the windows
2 cancel the newspapers
3 turn off the water and electricity
4 give your holiday address to the neighbours
5 ask the post office to forward your mail

On the plane, your friend thought about your advice. But he couldn't remember doing any of those things.

► *He couldn't remember **locking** the door.*

Continue...

130 irregular verbs (BEU 186)

Fill in the missing parts of these verbs.

Infinitive	Simple Past	Past Participle
awake		
		become
	broke	
bring		
catch		
		chosen
		fallen
	felt	
grow		
	kept	
know		
	laid	
	left	
		lain
	rode	
		risen
	shone	
		spent
steal		
	taught	
		worn

131 it's time (BEU 189.2)

Tell someone you know very well that it's time he/she did certain things.

► Your hair's greasy. **It's time** *you washed it.*

1 Your hair's too long.
2 You're too fat.
3 Your finger-nails are long.
4 Your shoes are dirty.
5 Your shirt's grubby.
6 Your socks smell.
7 Your room's untidy.
8 Your car's going rusty.
9 You owe me some money.
10 You've still got my dictionary.

137 **much**, **many**, **a lot** etc (BEU 205.1)

Do you eat or drink these things? How much?
Use *a lot of/lots of*, *many* or *much*.

▶ I eat **a lot of/lots of** vegetables.
I don't eat **many** vegetables.
I eat **a lot of** fish.
I don't eat **much** fish.

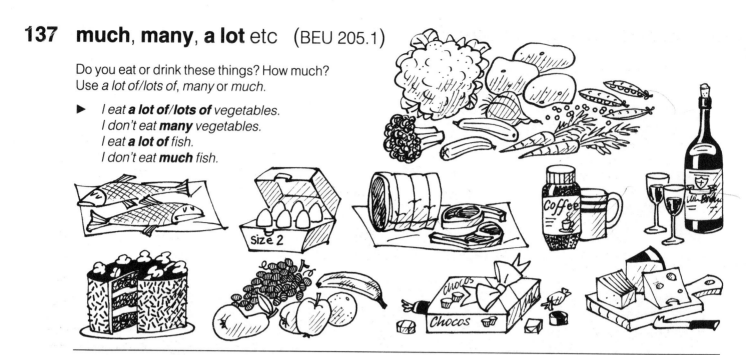

138 **must**: obligation (BEU 208)

I must. . .

▶ I've got an awful headache.
*I **must** take an aspirin.*

Continue. . .

1 My watch is broken.
2 My car's very dirty.
3 I've got a terrible cold
 and a cough.
4 I'm getting too fat.
5 I've got an awful toothache.

6 I smoke too many cigarettes.
7 I've got a pile of unpaid bills.
8 I've written three
 important letters.
9 My hair's too long.
10 The kitchen's in a mess.

139 **must**: obligation (BEU 208)

In national parks all over the world, you will find signs
similar to these. What mustn't you do?

▶ *You **mustn't** pick the flowers.*

1 140 **must**: deduction (BEU 210.1,2)

Who can they belong to?

▶ Who can the pipe belong to?
It can't belong to Liz or the children. It **must** *belong to Jim or Henry.*

145 nationality words (BEU 212)

Say what the people from some of these countries are famous for.

► *The **Austrians** are famous for their music.*
*The **French** make good wine.*

Countries		
Austria	Greece	Russia
China	Holland	Scotland
France	Italy	Switzerland
Germany	Japan	Thailand
the USA		

Ideas		
beer	cognac	silk
cameras	dancing	vodka
cars	food	watches
cheese	music	whisky
chocolate	perfume	wine

146 nationality words (BEU 212)

Can you match the country and the currency?
Use adjectives.

► *The **Austrian** schilling, the **Brazilian** cruzeiro, ...*

Austria	peseta
Brazil	pound
Britain	schilling
France	rupee
Greece	franc
India	krona
Italy	peso
Japan	lira
Mexico	drachma
Spain	yen
Sweden	dollar
USA	cruzeiro

147 need (BEU 213)

Put in *need, needn't, don't need, didn't need, needn't have* or *do ... need.*

1 You _____ worry about me. Everything's going to be fine.
2 I _____ worked so hard for the exam. It was much easier than I expected.
3 The flowers _____ some water. They're very dry.
4 _____ *(we)* to book a table at the restaurant, or are there usually enough places free?
5 You _____ bother to see me to the door, thanks. I know the way.
6 I _____ bought so much wine. Everybody drank beer!

7 You _____ tell me if it's a secret. I understand.
8 We _____ to check the figures again. I don't think they're right.
9 We _____ set off too early. The train doesn't leave until 9.30.
10 I met Mary by chance in town, so I _____ to ring her yesterday.
11 You _____ repair the toaster. I'll do it myself.
12 The window-cleaner came earlier than usual, so I _____ to clean them myself.

148 neither (BEU 217.1)

Compare the hotels, using *neither*.

▶ The Bridge Hotel hasn't got rooms with
a private bath.
Neither has the Woodland Hotel.

1 The Bridge Hotel isn't a 2-star.
2 The Bridge Hotel hasn't got rooms with television.
3 The Crown Hotel doesn't give reduced rates
for children.
4 The Bridge Hotel isn't open all the year round.
5 The Riverside Hotel hasn't got a bar.
6 The Crown Hotel doesn't offer free parking.
7 The Woodland Hotel hasn't got rooms with a
private bath.
8 The Woodland Hotel hasn't got rooms with
a telephone.
9 The Bridge Hotel hasn't got a lift.
10 The Woodland Hotel doesn't offer full board.

	Bridge Hotel	Crown Hotel	Riverside Hotel	Woodland Hotel
Cat.	★	★★	★★	★
🛁	−	15	12	−
CH	+	+	+	+
TV	−	+	+	−
☎	−	+	+	−
L	−	+	−	−
Y	−	+	−	−
FB	−	+	+	−
− %	+	−	−	+
P	−	−	−	+
O	−	+	−	−

Cat. = category   Y = bar
🛁 = bathroom   FB = full board
CH = central heating   − % = reduced rates
TV = television   for children
☎ = telephone   P = free parking
L = lift   O = open all year

149 neither... nor... (BEU 218)

Who didn't go where? A group of foreign students
went to London, but unfortunately they didn't have
enough time to see everything. Make sentences with
Neither . . . nor.

▶ **Neither** Ali **nor** Pablos went to Madame Tussaud's.

Continue. . .

Places to see	Tick the places you saw						
	Ali	Elena	Pablos	José	Kirsten	Pierre	Yasuko
Oxford Street	√		√	√	√		√
10 Downing Street	√	√		√		√	√
Westminster Abbey	√	√	√		√		√
St Paul's Cathedral	√		√	√		√	√
Houses of Parliament		√		√	√	√	√
The British Museum		√	√		√	√	√
The Tower of London	√	√	√	√	√		
The Tate Gallery	√		√		√	√	√
A pub	√	√	√	√		√	
Madame Tussaud's		√		√	√	√	√
Speaker's Corner	√	√	√		√		√

150 next and nearest (BEU 219)

next or *nearest*?

1 Excuse me, when's the _____ train to Dover, please?
2 I always shop at Savewell's supermarket – simply because it's the _____ .
3 The _____ bank is in the _____ street on the right.
4 'Which bus stop is the _____ to the hospital, please?' 'Duke Street. We're almost there. It's the _____ stop.'
5 'Where's the _____ phone-box, please?' 'There's one just round the corner. If it's not working, the _____ one's just across the park.'

6 Who sits _____ to you in class?
7 This post-box has already been emptied. Let's try the _____ one.
8 'What do you do in an emergency?' 'You get the patient to the _____ doctor.'
9 'Where's Station Road, please?' 'Keep straight on, then turn right at the _____ traffic lights.'

151 no and none (BEU 221)

no, none or *neither*?

1 _____ of us is perfect.
2 I have two brothers, but _____ of them lives here.
3 _____ child is good all the time.
4 'How many of the answers did you get right?' '_____ !'
5 The question was difficult. _____ of the pupils knew the answer.

6 I rang him yesterday, but there was _____ reply.
7 Unfortunately, there was _____ time left for questions.
8 _____ of my parents had a good education.
9 _____ kind of drug is harmless – however mild.
10 'Can you come to the theatre with us tonight?' 'Sorry! _____ time, _____ money!'

152 no and not (BEU 222)

no or *not*?

1 I could come on Saturday, but _____ on Sunday.
2 'What's the time, please?' 'Sorry, I've got _____ idea.'
3 _____ smoking in the bus, please, sir!
4 'Is that the truth?' 'Well, no, _____ exactly.'
5 _____ book can give you an answer to *that* question!

6 _____ talking during the examination, please!
7 It was margarine that you bought, _____ butter.
8 _____ surprisingly, he failed the examination.
9 _____ men were there. Only women.
10 There was _____ coffee, so I made tea.

153 numbers (BEU 227.1)

Say the answers aloud and write them in words.

▶ $\frac{4}{5} - \frac{7}{10} = \frac{1}{10}$ *(one tenth)*

a $\frac{3}{5} + \frac{1}{10} = ?$

b $\frac{2}{3} - \frac{1}{2} = ?$

c $\frac{3}{4} - \frac{1}{8} = ?$

d $\frac{1}{8} + \frac{1}{4} + \frac{3}{8} = ?$

e $\frac{1}{3} + \frac{5}{6} - \frac{1}{2} = ?$

f $\frac{4}{5} + \frac{3}{10} - \frac{1}{2} = ?$

154 numbers (BEU 227.4)

Here are the numbers of some useful telephone services in England:

Operator Service	dial	100
Emergency		999
Inland Director Enquiry Operator		192
Traveline		
Road, Rail, Sea and Air information		
Rail (InterCity and London Services)		01-246 8030
Road (Motorways and major roads)		01-246 8031
Sea		01-246 8032
Air		01-246 8033
Travel conditions within 70 miles of London		01-246 8021
Leisureline		
Main Daily Events in London		
In English		01-246 8041
In French		01-246 8043
In German		01-246 8045
Weatherline		
Local weather conditions		
In London Area		01-246 8091
South Kent and Sussex Coast		01-246 8097
Timeline		
In London	dial	123
Sportsline		
Up to date information on major sporting events		01-246 8020

Say aloud the number you would dial if . . .

1 . . . you wanted to know the exact time.
2 . . . you wanted to hear what's on in London in French.
3 . . . you needed an ambulance urgently.
4 . . . you needed an inland telephone number.
5 . . . you wanted to hear the weather report for London.
6 . . . you wanted to hear the Wimbledon tennis results.
7 . . . you needed to send a Telemessage through the operator.
8 . . . you wanted to hear the London theatre programmes in English.
9 . . . you needed InterCity train services.
10 . . . you wanted to know whether any airports are closed.

155 numbers (BEU 227.5)

Choose your answers from the list and say them aloud.

Elizabeth I, Elizabeth II, Charles I, Charles III, Henry VIII, George VI.

1 Who became Queen of England in 1952?
2 Who was her father?
3 When Prince Charles becomes king, what will his title be?
4 Which queen ruled England from 1558 to 1603?
5 Which king of England had six wives?
6 Which king of England was executed in 1649?

156 numbers (BEU 227.6)

On which floor would you get the following things? Which floor would it be if you were in an American department store?

1 a tie
2 writing paper
3 a tent
4 a handbag
5 a lamp
6 a plastic bowl
7 a tennis racket
8 a pair of jeans
9 a lipstick
10 something to eat

JOHNSON'S of London

Ground	1	2	3
Books & Records	Children's	Carpets	Camping
Cameras	Cosmetics	Fabrics	Electrical
Gift Shop	Furs	Gents' clothing	Furniture
Household goods	Jewellery	Ladies' clothing	Gardening
Leather goods	Shoes		Restaurant
Stationery			Sports

157 numbers (BEU 227.7)

How far is it. . . ? Say your answers aloud.

▶ . . . from New York to London?
It's five thousand, five hundred and thirty-six kilometres from New York to London.

1 . . . from Sydney to Johannesburg?
2 . . . from Tokyo to Buenos Aires?
3 . . . from London to Johannesburg?
4 . . . from New York to Sydney?
5 . . . from London to Tokyo?
6 . . . from Tokyo to New York?
7 . . . from Johannesburg to Buenos Aires?
8 . . . from Sydney to Tokyo?
9 . . . from Buenos Aires to London?

LONDON	London				
NEW YORK	5,536	New York			
BUENOS AIRES	11,129	8,539	Buenos Aires		
JOHANNES-BURG	9,067	12,822	8,109	Johannes-burg	
SYDNEY	17,007	16,003	11,755	11,019	Sydney
TOKYO	9,584	10,869	18,340	13,514	7,812

distances in kilometres

158 numbers (BEU 227.8)

1 Read aloud all the information on the cheque.
2 Write the following amounts in words:
£1,122 £127 £1,201 £2,135 £3,110

3 Draw another cheque and fill it in (you can decide yourself who the cheque is payable to, and how much it is for).

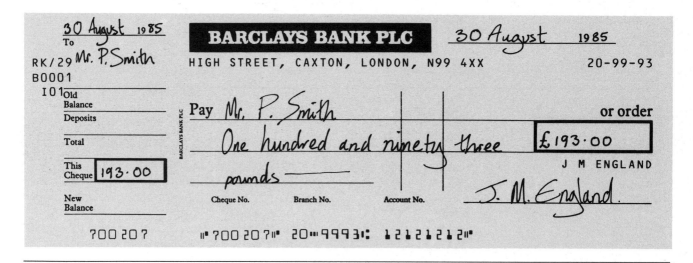

159 numbers (BEU 227.2,3,9)

The table shows the world's four top producers of road vehicles, in millions a year. How many do they make? Read the table aloud.

▶ *Japan produces two point four million lorries a year.*

	🚚	🚗	🏍
Japan	2.4m	4.5m	3.8m
USA	2.3m	6.5m	
USSR	0.8m		1.1m
UK	0.4m		
France		3.1m	1.0m
W. Germany		3.0m	
Italy			0.8m

160 numbers (BEU 227.10)

How much do you think they weigh?
Make sentences like this:

▶ *I think X weighs about _____ kilos.*

Mary   Julia   Bob   Sally

How tall do you think they are?
Make sentences like this:
▶ *I think X's about _____ feet
_____ (inches) tall.*

This will help:
2.5 cm = 1 inch
12 inches = 1 foot = about 30 cm

161 numbers (BEU 227.2,12)

▶ *On average, a three-year-old girl is ninety-six centimetres tall and weighs fourteen point five kilos.*

A three-year-old boy weighs fourteen point nine kilos and is ninety-seven centimetres tall.

Now continue to read the table aloud, as in the examples.

	Height in cm	Weight in kg	Age	Weight in kg	Height in cm	
	96	14.5	3	14.9	97	
	103	16.6	4	16.8	104	
	111	19.0	5	19.1	111	
	117	21.0	6	21.2	117	
	122	23.3	7	24.0	124	
	129	26.8	8	26.9	130	
	135	29.8	9	29.6	135	
	142	34.5	10	33.5	141	
	154	43.7	12	45.1	156	
	165	54.3	14	53.5	168	

162 one: substitute word (BEU 230)

Which *one/ones* would you like?

▶ *I'd like* **the one** *with the stripes/ the striped* **one**/**the one** *on the left* etc. (1)

1

2

3

4

5

6

7

8

9

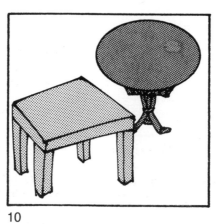

10

11

163 **ought** (BEU 232)

What *ought/oughtn't* they to do?

▶ I feel awfully tired.
   *You **ought** to have a sleep/go to bed.*
   *You **oughtn't** to work so hard/to go to bed so late.*

1 I don't feel well.
2 I've got a pain in my chest.
3 I think I'm short-sighted.
4 My tooth's aching again.
5 I have to get up very early tomorrow.

6 I'm putting on weight.
7 I lent a friend twenty pounds, but I haven't got it back.
8 My passport has expired.

Write about some more things that you ought to do.

164 **ought to have** (BEU 232.4)

Name six things that you ought to have done last week.

▶ *I **ought to have** written to my uncle.*
   *I **ought to have** repaired my bicycle.*

165 **own** (BEU 233.2)

Complete the sentences, using *of . . . own.*

▶ I usually borrow my brother's car. I can't afford a *car of my own.*

1 Jack shares a room with his brother. He'd rather have a _____ .
2 Mary shares a flat with another student. She'd prefer a _____ .
3 My parents live in a rented house. They'd like to have a _____ .
4 My friend often lends me his pocket calculator. I wish I had one _____ .
5 My sister and her husband have adopted a child. They couldn't have a child _____ .
6 My brother and I are allowed to use our parents' car, but we would both prefer to have a _____ .

7 David smoked my cigarettes all night. He didn't have any _____ .
8 Mark's father pays for all his studies, but Mark would prefer to have money _____ .
9 Aunt Susan always borrows my mother's sewing machine. She hasn't got one _____ .
10 My brother and I sometimes work in a local business. When we have enough money, we're going to open up a _____ .

166 participles used as adjectives (BEU 235)

Complete the sentences, using these adjectives.

boring	confusing	exciting
bored	confused	excited
frightening	interesting	tiring
frightened	interested	tired

SALLY   How did you enjoy the horror film? Was it very ___1___ ?

FRED   No, not particularly. But then I'd had a hard day, so I was feeling rather ___2___ . In fact, I almost fell asleep!

SALLY   Really? I'm always ___3___ by horror films! Was it at least ___4___ ?

FRED   Well, I didn't feel very ___5___ , not even at the end. We couldn't really understand what was happening. The story was ___6___ . Betty was ___7___ , too. Anyway, how was the party?

SALLY   Well, I'd had a very ___8___ day, too, and I didn't meet any ___9___ people, so I'm afraid I found it rather ___10___ .

FRED   Oh, I'm never ___11___ at parties. I'm always ___12___ in what's going on. Next time, you go to see the film and I'll go to the party!

167 participle clauses (BEU 236)

Rewrite, using a participle clause for the part in italics.

▶ *I didn't know what to do*, so I went home.
Not knowing what to do, I went home.

1 *Because I didn't know* who he was, I didn't speak to him.
2 She sat *and watched* the rain for hours.
3 *I needed some fresh air*, so I went jogging in the woods.
4 *After I had left you*, I went to the post office.
5 *Before you leave on holiday*, always make sure that the doors and windows are locked.
6 *All the people who are queueing over there* are hoping to get tickets for the football match.
7 *If it's properly looked after*, the engine will do another twenty thousand miles at least.
8 *Because he was rich*, he could afford a big house in the country.
9 *I looked at the menu* and found that the prices had gone up again.
10 *I wasn't in a hurry*, so I decided to walk to the office.
11 *He took a taxi* and managed to get to the station on time.
12 Who's that woman *who's talking to the postman*?

168 passive verb forms: simple present (BEU 238)

Name the main country/countries where the following are grown etc. Use the information in the table, and answer as in the examples. If you don't know, guess!

▶ *Cameras* **are manufactured** *in the USA and in Japan.*
Wheat **is grown** *in the USSR and in the USA.*

cameras
coffee
gold
maize
rice
ships
silk
tea
televisions
  & radios
tin
wheat
wine
wool
	build
	grow
	manufacture
	mine
	produce
		Australia
		Brazil
		China
		France
		India
		Japan
		Malaysia
		the USA
		the USSR
		South
		  Africa

169 passive verb forms: simple present (BEU 238)

How is bread made? Write out the text, using the following verbs: *cut, deliver, grind, harvest, leave, make, mix, pack, place, put, shape, slice, take* (×2)

In England, most bread *is made* from wheat. When the wheat is ripe, it __1__ . Then it __2__ to the flour mill. At the mill, it __3__ into flour. At the bread factory, first the flour __4__ with fat, salt, water and yeast to make a soft dough. When the dough has risen, it __5__ into pieces and the pieces __6__ into loaves. The loaves __7__ on big trays and __8__ in the oven to bake. After about an hour, the bread __9__ out and __10__ to cool. Then, some of the bread __11__ on a slicing-machine and __12__ into plastic bags. Finally, the bread __13__ to the shops in big vans.

170 passive verb forms: present progressive (BEU 238)

What's being done on the farm?

▶ *The hens **are being fed.*** (1)

Useful verbs: *clean out, collect, dry, feed, harvest, milk, plough, repair.*

1

2

3

4

5

6

7

8

9

10

11

174   **178**   past time: present perfect simple   (BEU 243.3)

What has happened? Say what has
happened in the following pictures.

► **She's won** the
   championship/cup.   (1)

1

2

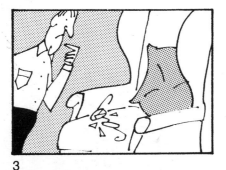

3

4

5

6

7

8

9

10

11

12

13

14

179 past time: present perfect simple (BEU 243.4,5)

Say which of these things
a   you have never done
b   you have already done
c   you haven't done yet
d   you have always wanted to do

speak to a famous person	win a large sum of money
be on television	buy a new car
have your fortune told	eat in a famous restaurant
see a James Bold film	visit London or New York
see a house on fire	
fall in love	

► *I've never spoken to a famous person.*
I've already seen a James Bond film.
I haven't been on television yet.
I've always wanted to visit London or New York.

Write about some other things that you have never done/already done/not done yet/always wanted to do.

---

180 past time: present perfect progressive (BEU 244.2)

What have they all been doing?

► *He's been playing football.* (1)

1

2

3

4

5

6

7

8

9

10

11

181 past perfect simple (BEU 245)

Olympic Games 1984

	Day 13		
	G	S	B
USA	63	53	27
Romania	18	14	11
China	15	7	7

	Day 14		
	G	S	B
USA	80	59	30
Romania	20	16	17
W. Germany	17	19	23

	Day 15		
	G	S	B
USA	83	61	30
Romania	20	16	17
W. Germany	17	19	23

The tables show the countries with the most medals on the last three days of the Olympic Games. Compare the tables like this:

▶ 13/Romania/gold
After day 13, Romania **had won** *18 gold medals.*

1 13/China/gold
2 14/W. Germany/gold
3 13/USA/gold
4 13/USA/silver
5 13/Romania/silver
6 13/China/silver

7 14/USA/gold
8 14/Romania/bronze
9 15/USA/gold
10 15/Romania/gold
11 15/W. Germany/gold
12 15/USA/silver

182 possessive 's (BEU 250.1)

Who is who?

▶ Who is Helen?
She is Jim's wife, Simon and Sally's mother,
Hilary and Paul's mother-in-law, the children's grandmother.

Who is Simon?
Who is Jim?
Who is Paul?
Who is Sally?
Who is Ben?

Helen   Jim

Hilary   Simon   Sally   Paul

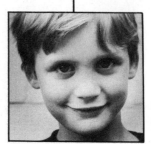

Susie   Ben

183 possessive 's (BEU 250.4)

Whose hat is it?

▶ *Hat number ten is John's.*

Now start with hat number one.

82

184 possessive 's (BEU 250.4)

Mrs Jones has bought all these things. Which shops has she been to? There isn't a supermarket in her part of the town.

▶ *She's been to the butcher's*.

185 possessives with determiners (**a friend of mine** etc) (BEU 252)

Kathy and John are cousins. Kathy and Mary are friends. John and Frank are colleagues. Frank and Kathy are friends. Kathy and Lucy are neighbours. Mr & Mrs Hill and Mary are neighbours.

▶ Does John know Kathy?
  *Yes, she's a cousin **of his***.

  Who's John?
  *He's a cousin **of Kathy's** and a colleague **of Frank's***.

1 Does Frank know John?
2 Does Mary know the Hills?
3 Does Kathy know Frank?
4 Does Lucy know Kathy?
5 Who's Mary?
6 Who's Frank?
7 Who's Lucy?
8 Who are the Hills?
9 Is Mary a friend of the Hills'?
10 Is Kathy a cousin of Frank's?

186 possessives: **mine** etc (BEU 253.2)

Four students share an unfurnished house. They have all bought some of the furniture and furnishings. Here's a list of what belongs to whom:

Ann	Charles	Sue and Helen (twins)
fridge	record player	curtains
television	bookshelves	6 chairs
iron	armchair	table
carpets	typewriter	oven
washing machine	radio	kitchen table
cutlery	sofa	cups and saucers
vacuum cleaner	electric kettle	pictures

▶ Does the armchair belong to Charles?
  *Yes, it's **his***.

1 Do the carpets belong to Ann?
2 Does the sofa belong to Charles?
3 Do the pictures belong to the twins?
4 Does the vacuum cleaner belong to Charles?
5 Does the typewriter belong to Ann?
6 Does the record player belong to the twins?
7 Does the radio belong to Charles?
8 Does the table belong to Ann?
9 Do the chairs belong to Charles?
10 Does the television belong to the twins?

187 prepositions at the end of clauses (BEU 257.1 d)

What do you need these things for?

▶ 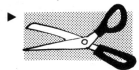 *You need scissors to cut* **with**.

1 2 3 4

5 6 7 8

9 10 11 12

---

188 present tenses: simple present (BEU 261.2)

Do you do any of these things? Be honest!
Answer as in the examples.

▶ ... watch rubbish on television?
Yes, I sometimes watch rubbish on television.
No, I never watch rubbish on television.

1 ... drop litter?
2 ... spend too much money on clothes?
3 ... have the radio on too loud?
4 ... neglect your homework/job?
5 ... criticize your teacher/boss behind his/her back?

6 ... tell little white lies?
7 ... ignore a traffic light?
8 ... forget your good manners?
9 ... think more of yourself than of others?
10 ... forget to pay your debts?

e they all doing?

Tom is putting up shelves. (1)

1 Tom

2 Kathy and Mike

3 Sue

4 Jerry

5 Sally and Ben

6 David

7 Jill

8 Barry

9 Diana

190 present tenses: present progressive (BEU 262.2)

An unexpected visitor comes to see you. It's very
noisy/very untidy in your house. Explain what's going
on. Begin: *'I'm sorry it's so noisy/untidy but. . . .'* Give
as many explanations as you can think of.

▶ *I'm sorry it's so noisy, but **we're having** a party/
but my brother**'s playing** his jazz records.*

*I'm sorry it's so untidy, but **we're moving** the
furniture/but **I'm cleaning out** drawers.*

---

191 progressive tenses with **always** (BEU 263)

What are they always doing?

▶ an absent-minded person **is always
forgetting** things.

1	a trouble-maker	6	a gossip
2	an egoist	7	a spoil-sport
3	a clumsy person	8	a pessimist
4	a liar	9	a vain person
5	a hypochondriac	10	a tell-tale

---

192 questions (BEU 270)

You meet a young American who is staying in your
town. You have a lot of questions. Here are the answers.
What are the questions?

▶ I come from California.
Where do you come from?
or
Where are you from?

1 I arrived last Sunday.
2 For three weeks.
3 I came by plane and train.
4 At a small hotel in the town.
5 Yes, it's my first time here.

6 Yes, I like it very much.
7 No, I haven't seen that yet.
8 No, I'm afraid I can't speak your language at all.
9 Yes, I do. I like the food very much.
10 No, I haven't been there yet.

---

193 question tags (BEU 273)

You're speaking to someone you have met for the first
time. You have heard several things about him/her
from a friend. Find out if it's all true.

▶ He/She is English.
*You're English, **aren't you**?*

You have heard that:

1 He/She is a computer specialist.
2 He/She has been to your country before.
3 He/She is staying for three months.
4 He/She works for an American company.
5 He/She used to work for an English company.

6 He/She knows a few words of your language.
7 He/She would like to learn the language properly.
8 He/She was on holiday in your country last year.
9 He/She doesn't like the food very much.
10 He/She can play tennis very well.

194 reflexive pronouns (BEU 276.2)

Who does it? Answer with *myself, yourself* etc, as in the example.

► Do you always go to the hairdresser's?
Yes, I never/hardly ever/cut my hair **myself**.
No, I sometimes do/cut my hair **myself**.

1 Do you iron your own clothes?
2 Does your father/husband have his car repaired at a garage?
3 Do you shop for food yourself?
4 Do you decorate your house/flat yourselves?
5 Do your parents/neighbours clean their house/flat themselves?

6 Do you wash your clothes yourself?
7 Does your mother/wife/girlfriend go to the hairdresser's?
8 Does your father/husband repair things in the house himself?
9 Do you wash your car yourself/yourselves?
10 Did your mother/wife make the curtains herself?

---

195 relative pronouns: **who** (BEU 277)

Describe the pupils in this old school photo.

► *Jane's the girl* **who** *was very good at sports.*

196 relative pronouns: **that**   (BEU 277.2)

Do you know the answers? Choose from the names in
the box. If you don't know, guess!

▶ river/flows from Switzerland to the Netherlands?
   *The river **that** flows from Switzerland to the
   Netherlands is the Rhine.*

Sri Lanka	Singapore	USSR
Venezuela	Hong Kong	San Marino
India	Brasilia	Canada
Iceland	Monaco	Rio de Janeiro
Greenland	Peru	

1 tiny country/lies in the middle of Italy?
2 part of China/is leased to Britain until 1997?
3 Danish island/lies in the Arctic?
4 country/has more coastline than any other
   country?
5 city/has the world's largest football stadium?
6 island/lies at the southern point of India?
7 country/has the highest waterfall in the world?
8 country/covers a sixth of all the land in the world?
9 city/was built specially to be a new capital, about
   30 years ago?
10 country/has the most languages?

197 relatives: **whose**   (BEU 279)

You want to know who these people are. Begin: *Who's the man whose...?*

▶ *Who's the man **whose** trousers are too big for him?*

Continue...

198 relatives: identifying clauses (BEU 280)

Describe the rooms in a house. Say what you do in them. Leave out the relative pronoun, as in the examples.

▶ the bedroom
The bedroom is the room/place you sleep in.

1	the bathroom	6	the nursery
2	the dining room	7	the guest room
3	the kitchen	8	the attic
4	the sitting room	9	the cellar
5	the study	10	the garage

---

199 reported speech: tenses (BEU 283.3)

Mary B., age 14, wrote this letter to a women's magazine. What did she write/say?

▶ *She wrote that she was 14 and felt confused as to when she became an adult.*

Continue...

I am 14 and feel confused as to when I become an adult. I can get married at 16, but I can't vote until I'm 18! At the cinema I already pay for an adult ticket, but I'm not allowed to see 'adult' films! I can drive a car at 17, but on the bus and tube I start paying adult fares at 15! Travel companies and many airlines offer reductions for children under 12. The age when I become an adult seems to depend on where I'm sitting!

Mary B., London SE 3

---

200 reported speech: tenses (BEU 283.3)

In many countries, it has become compulsory to wear car seat-belts. Many people are for this, some are against it. Here are some opinions. What did they all say?

▶ *Pat Swindon said that she was glad....*

Continue...

Pat Swindon, 26, secretary:
'I'm glad that seat-belts have become compulsory. I'm sure that the number of road deaths will drop.'

Bill Brown, 19, apprentice:
'I hate wearing a seat-belt. I don't feel free. I don't intend to use it in future. I just hope that I don't get caught by the police.'

Patrick Marshall, 30, computer specialist:
'I'm in favour of wearing seat-belts. I always fasten mine. I always did and I always will do.'

Jane Wilson, 24, nurse:
'I see what terrible accidents happen to people who don't wear seat-belts. I hope that belts for the back seats will also become compulsory.'

201 reported speech: questions (BEU 284)

What do they want to know?

▶ *Doris G. wants to know how much notice she must give.*

Continue. . .

Dear Sue,   Doris G.
I want to leave my present
job as a typist. How much
notice must I give? I have

Dear Sue,   Pam E.
                                    Surrey
How can I get my boyfriend
to stop smoking? He never

Dear Sue,   John K.
Should I tell my teacher that
I've fallen in love with her?
I know it would ca...
but I feel u...
th...
fin...
May...
who...

David B.

Dear Sue,
When can I legally leave
home? I can't possibly

Barry G.

Dear Sue,
Why does my girlfriend
tell me lies? My problem
...the fact that

Kathy P.

Dear Sue,
Should I marry a man who's
thirty years older than me?
...not worried about
...in years

Mary M.

Dear Sue
How can I get rid of my
spots? I have been to

Roger A.

Dear Sue,
Why haven't I made any friends
at my new school?
I am friendl
so l...

Lucy L.

Dear Sue,
Why do people treat me
like a child? I'm 16 years
old and I have just got

Patricia H.

Dear Sue,
My boss has invited me to a party
Should I go? The party will be

Dear Sue,   Diane B.
I have broken my engagement.
Do I have to give back my
engagement ring?

SUE'S PROBLEM PAGE

206 short answers (BEU 293.1)

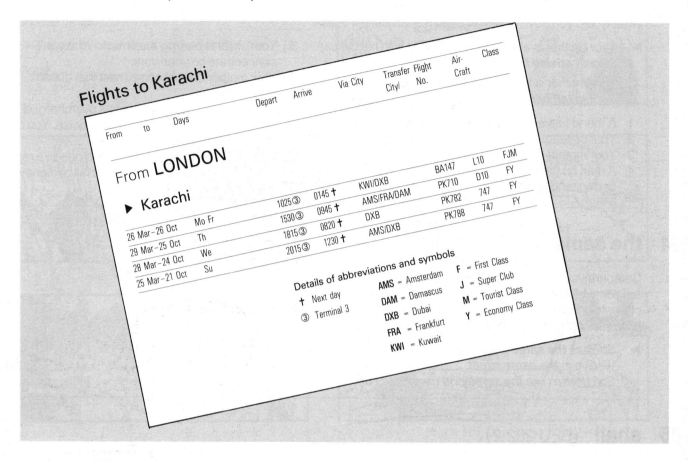

Flights to Karachi

From	to	Days	Depart	Arrive	Via City	Transfer City/	Flight No.	Air-Craft	Class
From LONDON									
▶ **Karachi**							BA147	L10	FJM
26 Mar – 26 Oct		Mo Fr	1025③	0145 †	KWI/DXB		PK710	D10	FY
29 Mar – 25 Oct		Th	1530③	0945 †	AMS/FRA/DAM		PK782	747	FY
28 Mar – 24 Oct		We	1815③	0820 †	DXB		PK788	747	FY
25 Mar – 21 Oct		Su	2015③	1230 †	AMS/DXB				

Details of abbreviations and symbols

† Next day
③ Terminal 3

AMS = Amsterdam
DAM = Damascus
DXB = Dubai
FRA = Frankfurt
KWI = Kuwait

F = First Class
J = Super Club
M = Tourist Class
Y = Economy Class

▶ Do all flights go via Dubai?
No, they don't.

Is there a flight on Wednesday?
Yes, there is.

1 Do all flights depart from Terminal 3?
2 Are there any non-stop flights?
3 Does the Sunday flight go via Kuwait?
4 Do the 747 flights go via Dubai?
5 Has flight BA147 got a Super Club class?
6 Is there a flight that leaves in the morning?
7 Does the British Airways flight go twice a week?

8 Is there a flight on Tuesday?
9 Have the Pakistan International flights all got an Economy class?
10 Is there a Pakistan International flight via Frankfurt?
11 Do all flights arrive on the next day?
12 Is there a daily flight?

207 short answers (BEU 293.2)

Give short answers in reply to these statements.

▶ You've got dark hair.
Yes, I have. No, I haven't.

1 You're over 18.
2 You've got brown eyes.
3 You like school/work.
4 You've got long hair.
5 You speak English.

6 You usually get up late.
7 You're shy.
8 You're wearing jeans.
9 You went out last night.
10 You were late for school/work this morning.

208 should (BEU 294)

Several things are in the wrong rooms. Where should they be?

▶   *The fridge **shouldn't** be in the bathroom. It **should** be in the kitchen.*

Continue. . .

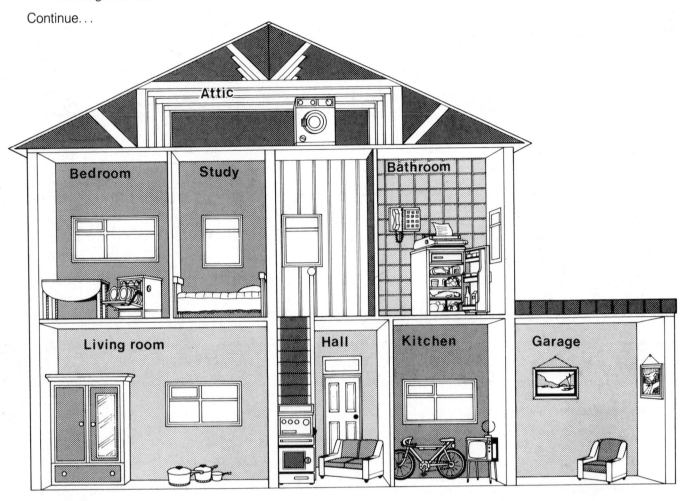

209 should (BEU 294.2)

Use *should* and *shouldn't*. What would you say to a
friend who. . .

1   eats too many sweets?
2   has lost his wallet?
3   has an old car that's always being repaired?
4   is too fat?
5   spends too much money on clothes?
6   has lost his job?
7   has got a girlfriend that spends all his money?
8   has bought a record that's scratched?

What advice could your friends give <u>you</u>?

210 **since** (conjunction of time): tenses (BEU 300)

Answer with *since* and the present perfect or past tense.

▶ How long have you known your best friend?
*I've known my best friend **since** we were at school.*

How long have you known your neighbours?
*I've known my neighbours **since** I've been in this street.*

1 How long have you known your best friend?
2 How long have you known your neighbours?
3 How long have you known your best friend's family?
4 How long have you known your class teacher/boss?
5 How long have you known your English teacher?

6 How long have you known your boyfriend/ girlfriend/partner?
7 How long have you known your doctor?
8 How long have you known your dentist?
9 How long have you known your butcher?

211 spelling of plural nouns (BEU 301)

What was on the shopping list? Fill in the missing words.

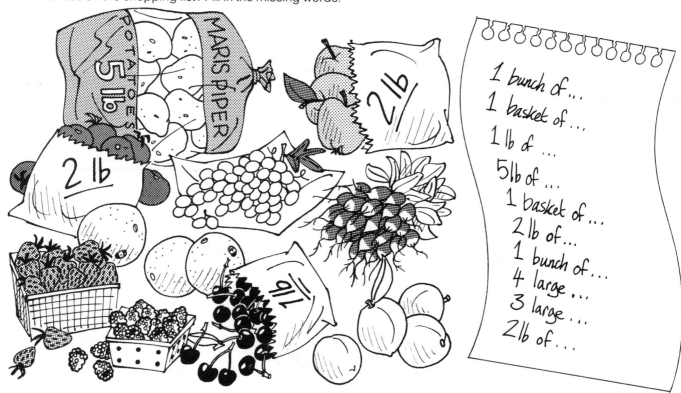

1 bunch of ...
1 basket of ...
1 lb of ...
5 lb of ...
1 basket of ...
2 lb of ...
1 bunch of ...
4 large ...
3 large ...
2 lb of ...

212 **so** and **not** with **hope**, **believe** etc (BEU 311)

Give suitable short answers with *so* and *not*. Use *be afraid, believe, expect, hope, suppose, think.*

▶ Are you a good cook?
*I think **so**./I suppose **so**./I hope **so**./I'm afraid **not**.*

1 Are you reliable?
2 Are you a bad loser?
3 Are you overanxious?
4 Are you vain?
5 Are you a bore?
6 Do people enjoy your company?
7 Are you a good singer?

8 Are you a good friend to have?
9 Are you a careful person?
10 Do people complain about you for any reason?
11 Are you successful?
12 Have you got all these answers right?

213 **so am I**, **so do I** etc (BEU 312)

Study the application forms and compare the candidates.

▶ *Mary lives in Manchester. **So does** Diana.*
*Diana has five O-levels. **So have** Mary and Susan.*

Application Form
Name: *Diana Clark*
Address: *2, Park Road, Manchester*
Date of birth: *23 July 1964*
Country of birth: *England*
Qualifications: *Maths, History, Geography, English, French (O-levels)*
Shorthand: *100 words per minute*
Typing: *50 words per minute*
Experience: *4 years shorthand typist*
Hobbies: *Cooking, Reading*
Sports: *Tennis, Squash*

Application Form
Name: *Mary Jones*
Address: *14 Hill Street, Manchester*
Date of birth: *30 September 1965*
Country of birth: *Scotland*
Qualifications: *O-Levels: English, Maths, Music, Geography, French*
Shorthand: *120 words per minute*
Typing: *50 words per Minute*
Experience: *3 years junior secretary*
Hobbies: *Music, Reading, Dancing*
Sports: *Swimming, Climbing*

Application Form
Name: *Susan Higgins*
Address: *122, MILL ROAD, LIVERPOOL*
Date of birth: *1 JULY 1964*
Country of birth: *SCOTLAND*
Qualifications: *O LEVELS IN ENGLISH, MATHS, BIOLOGY, FRENCH, ART*
Shorthand: *100 WORDS PER MINUTE*
Typing: *40 WORDS PER MINUTE*
Experience: *SHORTHAND TYPIST 4 YEARS*
Hobbies: *DANCING, READING, COOKING*
Sports: *SWIMMING, TENNIS*

214 **some** and **any** (BEU 314)

What's left after the party? Begin: *There's **some**...,*
*There isn't **any**..., There's **hardly any**...,*
*There aren't **any**..., There are **hardly any**...*

▶ *There's **some** coffee.*

215 **somebody** and **anybody**, **something** and **anything** etc (BEU 317)

Put in *somebody, something, somewhere, anybody, anything, anywhere.*

1 'Where's the dog? I can't find him _____ .'
  'Well, he must be _____ . Look down the road.'
2 'There's _____ called Smith on the phone for you.'
  'Smith? I don't know _____ by that name.'
3 'I'm going into town today. Is there _____ I can get for you?'
  'No, thanks. I don't need _____ .'
4 I'm looking for _____ , but I can't find it _____ .

5 'Do you know _____ about education in China?'
  'No, not much.'
6 _____ has taken my raincoat by mistake.
7 Let's go _____ nice on Sunday, shall we?
8 'Where did you find this lovely old lamp?' 'In an antique shop _____ in Portland Road.'
9 I'm doing a crossword puzzle. Does _____ want to help me?
10 Have you been _____ exciting this week?

---

216 **still**, **yet** and **already** (BEU 330)

still, yet or *already*?

1 'Has the postman been _____ ?' 'No, he's _____ chatting to the neighbour.'
2 You needn't wash the dishes. I've _____ done them.
3 'Has it stopped raining _____ ?' 'No, not _____ .
4 'I'm going to Bangkok next month.' 'Oh, you'll enjoy it. I've _____ been there.'
5 'Have you finished your homework _____ ?' 'No, I'm _____ doing it.'

6 She's _____ arrived. The train was early.
7 'Where's John? Has he _____ left?' 'No, not _____ . He's _____ in his office.'
8 He's _____ left Caracas but he hasn't reached Quito _____ .
9 'Have you finished your report _____ ?', 'No, I'm _____ writing it, I'm afraid.'
10 I haven't done the housework _____ . I'm _____ writing letters.

---

217 subject and object forms (BEU 331.1)

Who likes whom?

▶ *I like Jeff, but he doesn't like me.*

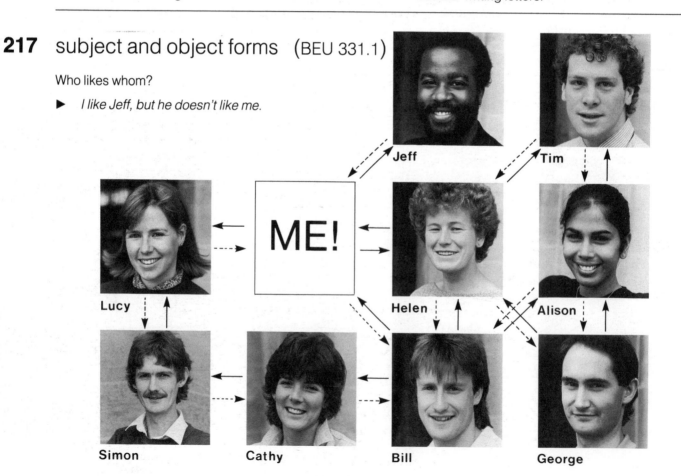

218 **such** and **so** (BEU 334)

such or *so*?

1 He's _____ a nice person. I'm sure you'll like him.
2 She's _____ stubborn. She never takes advice from anyone.
3 I really enjoyed the play. It was _____ a good performance.
4 She's not pretty, but she's got _____ lovely eyes.
5 Don't have dinner there. They serve _____ bad food that you can't eat it.
6 Our teacher's very nice. He's got _____ patience.
7 The box is _____ heavy that I can hardly lift it.
8 The countryside is _____ beautiful here!
9 The book's _____ exciting that I can't put it down!
10 He's _____ clever. He knows the answer to everything!

219 **take** (time) (BEU 338)

How long does it usually take you to do the following?

▶ to do the shopping?
It **takes** me about an hour.
It sometimes **takes** ages!
It doesn't usually **take** long.

1 to get to school/work?
2 to write a letter in English?
3 to walk/run a kilometre?
4 to clean your car/bicycle?
5 to clean your shoes?

How long did the following take (you)?

▶ the above sentences?
They didn't **take** long.
They **took** me ages!
They **took** me about 5 minutes.

6 the journey/walk to school/work this morning?
7 the last exercise you did from this book?
8 breakfast this morning?
9 your morning shower/bath?
10 to learn to pronounce English well?

220 telling the time (BEU 342.1,2)

What time do you usually do the following?

▶ get up during the week?
I usually get up at half past seven (seven thirty) during the week.

1 get up during the week?
2 get up on Sundays?
3 go to bed during the week?
4 go to bed at the weekend?
5 have breakfast?
6 leave home in the morning?
7 arrive home from school/work?
8 have lunch on Sunday?
9 have your evening meal?
10 watch the news on television?

221 **there is** (BEU 345.1)

What is there where? Ask questions and answer them, as in the examples.

pandas	oil	windmills
tea	diamonds	pyramids
coffee	iron	penguins
kangaroos	kiwis	rice
polar bears	alligators	wheat

▶ penguins/the Arctic?
Are there penguins in the Arctic?
No, there aren't, but there are polar bears in the Arctic.

rice/Britain?
Is there rice in Britain?
No, there isn't, but there's wheat in Britain.

1 windmills/Egypt?
2 kiwis/China?
3 kangaroos/River Amazon?
4 tea/Brazil?
5 pyramids/Holland?
6 iron/Iran?
7 diamonds/Sweden?
8 alligators/Australia?
9 pandas/New Zealand?
10 oil/South Africa?

222 **until** and **by** (BEU 351); **until** and **to** (BEU 352)

until, by or *to*?

1 I'd like to stay _____ Monday, if that's OK.
2 If you want to catch the 3.30 train, you'll have to leave the house _____ 3 o'clock at the latest.
3 We waited _____ half past eight, but he didn't come.
4 The garage mechanic said he could have the car finished _____ Thursday.
5 'How far did you walk?' '_____ the river and back.'

6 How long is it _____ Christmas?
7 I only work from nine _____ two on Fridays.
8 We're getting up very early tomorrow, so we'll have to be in bed _____ 9 o'clock tonight.
9 Can you wait _____ I come back? I'll only be 5 minutes.
10 The television's broken. We hoped to have it back _____ the weekend, but the shop said they'd have to keep it _____ Wednesday.

223 **used to** + infinitive (BEU 353)

What did there use to be? Compare the plans like this:

▶ There **used to be** a cinema in Duke Street. Now it's a supermarket.
There **didn't use to be** a bus stop in Church Street.

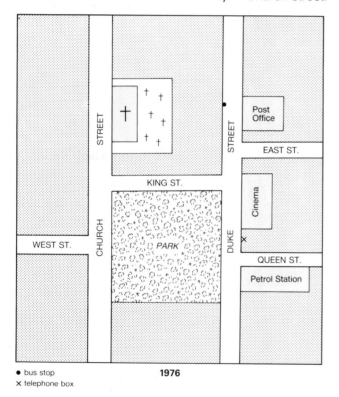

1976

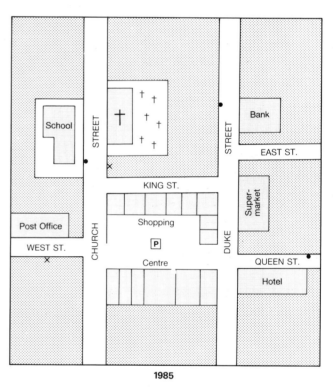

1985

● bus stop
✕ telephone box

224 **(be) used to** + . . .-ing (BEU 354)

Which of these things are you used to doing, and which are you not used to doing?

▶ I'm **used to** getting up early.
I'm **not used to** driving long distances.

working hard	living in a big city
going to bed late	spending a lot of time alone
getting up early	lying in the sun for hours
eating spicy foods	travelling abroad a lot
walking long distances	looking after small children
driving long distances	riding a bicycle

225　verbs with two objects　(BEU 356.1)

Say what you *bought, gave, made* or *sent* different
people for recent birthdays and special occasions.

▶　*I bought my friend a record for his birthday.*
I made my little sister a wooden doll for Christmas.

226　**when** and **if**　(BEU 360);　**whether** and **if**　(BEU 361)

when or *if* (or both)? *whether* or *if* (or both)?

1　I'm going to town this afternoon. _____ I see a
chemist's, I'll get you some aspirins.
2　I'll see you on the 6.30 bus – _____ I get up
early enough!
3　I'm going to Bristol in the morning. I'll ring you
_____ I get there.
4　We discussed _____ or not we should agree to
the plan.
5　Perhaps I'll fly to Caracas in the autumn. _____ I
do, I'll visit you.

6　Ask him _____ he wants to come with us.
7　Please let me know _____ you are coming on
Friday or not.
8　_____ you boil water, it turns to steam.
9　_____ you know the answer, say so; _____ not,
just keep quiet and hope you won't get asked!
10　_____ I go to London next time, I'll stay at a
better hotel.

227　**whoever**, **whatever**, **whichever**, **however**, **whenever**, **wherever**　(BEU 365)

Put in whichever is suitable.

1　_____ you do, don't give him the money!
2　'When do you want me to come?' '_____ you like!'
3　You'll enjoy Austria. It's lovely _____ you go.
4　'Which is my seat?' 'You can sit _____ you like.'
5　_____ answers the phone, tell them I'm not here!
6　He'll never be clever, _____ hard he works.

7　'You can take _____ books you like.' 'I don't
need any of them.'
8　_____ I see a plane, I always feel like going
on holiday!
9　He takes his little brother with him _____ he goes.
10　Please say I'm out, _____ asks for me!

228　**wish**　(BEU 367.2)

Kate and Paul have regrets. What do they wish?

▶　*Kate **wishes** she didn't smoke. Paul **wishes** he had gone to university.*

Continue...

I smoke.
I've bought so many new clothes.
I can't handle money.
I don't speak a foreign language.
I wasted too much time at school.
I've spent all my savings.
I don't take life seriously.
I haven't got a steady boyfriend.
Paul didn't ask me out.

I didn't go to university.
I didn't become a teacher.
I didn't work hard enough at school.
I haven't got a car.
I can't dance.
I'm shy.
I don't make friends easily.
I'm not interested in sport.
I didn't dare to ask Kate out.

229 worth . . .-ing (BEU 368)

What is it worth doing? Add comments using *worth . . .-ing* with a suitable verb, as in the examples.

▶ Vienna is a beautiful city. *It's worth visiting.*
This radio's broken. *It isn't worth repairing.*

1 'Dr Zhivago' is a good film.
2 These old shoes are shabby.
3 British stamps are very attractive.
4 This old book may be valuable.
5 'Gone with the Wind' is an interesting book.

6 Second-hand TV sets often break down.
7 China is a very interesting country.
8 A good education is important.
9 These old letters and postcards are no good.
10 This is a good record.

230 would rather (BEU 370.2)

You would prefer your girlfriend/boyfriend/husband/ wife to do or not to do the following things. Begin with *I'd rather. . .*, as in the examples.

▶ You would prefer him/her to save more money.
I'd rather you saved more money.

You would prefer him/her not to smoke.
I'd rather you didn't smoke.

You would prefer him/her. . .

1 to take life more seriously
2 not to wear old jeans all the time
3 not to buy you so many presents
4 not to work on Saturdays
5 to have his/her hair cut
6 not to drive so fast
7 not to criticize your friends
8 to stop spending money on clothes
9 not to waste so much time on the phone
10 to work a bit harder

Key

Key

1

(Possible answers)
2 The sports car's about to overtake the lorry.
3 The old man's about to cross the road.
4 The shoppers are about to get on (to) the bus.
5 The little girl's about to press the button.
6 The boys are about to get on (to) their motorbikes.
7 The van's about to go round/turn the corner.
8 The dog's about to run across the road.
9 The little boy's about to get on (to) his bicycle.
10 The policemen are about to get into the police car.
11 The taxi-driver's about to drive off.

2

1 over 2 over 3 Above 4 above/over 5 over
6 above 7 over 8 above 9 above 10 over

3

1 through 2 across 3 through 4 across 5 across/
over 6 across/over 7 through 8 across 9 over
10 over

4

(Possible answers)
She had *completely* forgotten the time. She *quietly* turned the key in the door. But how strange – it wasn't *even* locked. Had she *really* forgotten to lock the door? Perhaps she had. *Nevertheless*, a strange feeling came over her. (*Suddenly*) her heart (*suddenly*) started beating *loudly*. She (*nervously*) pushed the door open (*nervously*) and listened. She heard a noise *upstairs*. It had *definitely* come from the bedroom. *At first* she didn't know what to do. There was *obviously* someone in the house. She must think *clearly* what to do. She knew that she must ring the police *at once*. She (*silently*) moved (*silently*) towards the phone. *Then* she remembered that it was out of order. (*The morning before*) she had tried to phone her brother (*the morning before*). She groped her way back to the door. *Unfortunately* there was a china vase *on the hall table*. She brushed against it.

5

(Suggestions)
1 Yes, there's always snow in winter. No, there's never snow in winter.
2 Yes, it's sometimes foggy. No, it's rarely foggy.
3 Yes, there is often heavy rainfall in summer. No, there's rarely heavy rainfall in summer.
4 Yes, it's occasionally hotter than 30°C. No, it's never hotter than 30°C.
5 Yes, there are sometimes thunderstorms. No, there are rarely thunderstorms.
6 Yes, you can sometimes sunbathe in winter. No, you can never sunbathe in winter.
7 Yes, it's always humid. No, it's rarely humid.
8 Yes, the temperature is occasionally below freezing point. No, the temperature is never below freezing point.
9 Yes, there are sometimes floods. No, there are never floods.
10 Yes, there is occasionally a hurricane in our area. No, there's never a hurricane in our area.

6

(Suggestions)
1 On Sundays I always go for a walk.
2 After school/work I often meet my friends.
3 During the week I seldom go out.
4 At weekends I never watch television.
5 In summer I frequently go swimming.
6 In winter I rarely play tennis.
7 On holiday I sometimes take photographs.
8 On Sunday mornings I usually read the papers.
9 When it rains I normally clean the house.
10 In the evenings I occasionally go to the cinema.

7

(Suggestions)
1 Yes, I cook well. No, I don't cook well./No, I cook badly.
2 Yes, I work hard. No, I don't work hard.
3 Yes, I learn fast. No, I don't learn fast./No, I learn slowly.
4 Yes, I speak English fluently. No, I don't speak English fluently.
5 Yes, I sing well. No, I don't sing well./No, I sing badly.
6 Yes, I smoke heavily. No, I don't smoke heavily.
7 Yes, I run fast. No, I don't run fast./No, I run slowly.
8 Yes, I dance well. No, I don't dance well./No, I dance badly.
9 Yes, I drive carefully. No, I don't drive carefully./No, I drive carelessly.
10 Yes, I play tennis well. No, I don't play tennis well./No, I play tennis badly.

8

Today. She has to see Brenda in the canteen at 12.30. She has to go to the dentist's at 2.15. She has to pick up Roger at King's Cross Station at 5.30. She's going to a jazz concert at the Cavern Club at 7.30.
Tuesday. She's going to town with Sarah in the afternoon. She's going to a disco at 8 pm.
Wednesday. She's going for an interview at the Sun Travel Agency at 9.15. She's going to a concert at the Central Hall at 8 pm.
Thursday. She's going to Manchester at 8.15 am. She's meeting Sally at the airport at about 6.30 pm.

9

(Possible answers)
On Monday afternoon, after visiting Westminster Abbey, they went to the Houses of Parliament./. . . they visited Westminster Abbey and afterwards they went to the Houses of Parliament.
On Monday evening, after seeing 'The Mousetrap', they had a meal at/in a Chinese restaurant./. . . they saw 'The Mousetrap' and afterwards they had a meal at/in a Chinese restaurant.
On Tuesday morning, after going to Madame Tussaud's, they visited the Planetarium./. . . they went to Madame Tussaud's and afterwards they visited the Planetarium.
On Tuesday afternoon, after looking round/visiting Windsor Castle, they took a walk through Windsor./. . . they looked round/visited Windsor Castle and afterwards they went for a walk through Windsor.
On Tuesday evening, after having/going for a boat ride on the Thames, they had a meal at a steak house./. . . they had/went for a boat ride on the Thames and afterwards they had a meal at a steak house.
On Wednesday morning, after doing some shopping in Oxford Street, they had lunch at/in an Italian restaurant./. . . they did some shopping in Oxford Street and afterwards they had lunch at/in an Italian restaurant.
On Wednesday afternoon, after looking round/visiting the British Museum, they had a few beers in a nearby pub./. . . they looked round/visited the British Museum and afterwards they had a few beers in a nearby pub.
On Wednesday evening, after going to a concert at the Queen Elizabeth Hall, they had supper at/in an Indian restaurant./. . . they went to a concert at the Queen Elizabeth Hall and afterwards they had supper at/in an Indian restaurant.
On Thursday morning, after visiting 10 Downing Street, they

went walking/for a walk in Hyde Park./ . . . they visited 10 Downing Street and afterwards they went walking/for a walk in Hyde Park.

On Thursday afternoon, after looking round/visiting the Tate Gallery, they went to a coffee-shop./ . . . they looked round/ visited the Tate Gallery and afterwards they went to a coffee-shop.

10
1 for   2 before   3 ago   4 for   5 ago   6 for
7 before   8 ago   9 for   10 before

11
1 all/everything   2 all   3 everything   4 All   5 all
6 everything   7 every   8 everybody   9 all   10 All
11 Everybody   12 all

12
1 Although I eat a lot, I'm not fat.
2 Although I get up late, I'm seldom late for work.
3 Although I drink a lot of beer, I'm never drunk.
4 Although I drive badly, I've never had an accident.
5 Although I don't look after my car, it runs well.
6 Although I spend a lot of money, I'm not in debt.
7 Although I don't go to the dentist's, my teeth are healthy.

13
another cup of tea   another piece of chocolate cake
some more sugar   some more apple pie
another sandwich   some more cream
two more biscuits   another piece of fruit cake
some more milk   some more strawberry gâteau

14
1 the   2 a   3 a   4 The   5 a   6 the   7 a   8 the
9 the   10 a   11 the   12 the   13 the   14 the   15 the
16 the

15
(Suggestions)
1 I go to work at . . .
2 I live in the town/the country.
3 I eat . . . for breakfast.
4 I go to school/work by bus/by bicycle/on foot.
5 I play/don't play the piano/the guitar.
6 I prefer the mountains/the sea.
7 I prefer to go on holiday in (the) spring/in (the) summer.
8 Yes, I often lie/No, I don't often lie in the sun.
9 Yes, I've been/No, I haven't been in hospital.
10 I watch television . . .

16
(Suggestions)
1 The Nile
2 Narita Airport
3 The Dead Sea, Lake Titicaca
4 The Pyrenees
5 The Matterhorn, Mount Fuji, Citlaltepetl
6 The Pacific
7 The Sorbonne, Coimbra University
8 The Ramblas, Vasilissis Sofias Avenue
9 The Ritz
10 The Gare du Nord, Padua Station

17
Pam's an air hostess.   Pat's a nurse.
Mike's an author.   Bill's an actor.
Jim's a mechanic.   Tom's a translator.
Jeff's an electrician.   Mark's a shop assistant.
Joe's an architect.

18
1 Mary's as tall as Pat, but she isn't as tall as Pam.
2 Dick smokes as many cigarettes as Peter, but he doesn't smoke as many as Tom.
3 Susan works as long as Jane, but she doesn't work as long as Jill.
4 Peter earns as much as Dick, but he doesn't earn as much as Tom.
5 Uncle Stan weighs as much as Uncle Dan, but he doesn't weigh as much as Uncle Sam.
6 Susan gets up as early as Jane, but she doesn't get up as early as Jill.

19
1 like   2 as   3 as/like   4 like   5 like   6 like   7 as
8 like   9 as/like   10 as

20
As/When/While I was cleaning the floor, the dog knocked over the bucket of water.
As/When/While I was phoning my aunt, the phone went dead.
As/When/While I was unlocking the car, I dropped the keys down a drain.
As/When/While I was running for the bus, my hat blew off.
As/When/While I was pushing a trolley round the supermarket, I knocked down a stack of tins.
As/When/While I was looking in a shop window, somebody stole my purse.
As/When/While I was cooking lunch, the electricity went off.
As/When/While I was putting a cake in the oven, I burnt my arm.
As/When/While I was turning a sharp corner, I fell off my bicycle.
As/When/While I was watching the news, the television broke down.

21
1 –/for   2 for   3 –   4 –   5 for   6 for   7 –   8 for   9 –
10 –

22
(Possible answers)
1 on an ambulance
2 at the customs
3 on woollen clothing
4 on a Mercedes car
5 at an airport
6 in an aeroplane
7 at the cinema, in an aeroplane
8 on a box
9 at the cinema, in an aeroplane, in a shop
10 on a garden gate
11 in a park
12 in a museum, in a shop
13 at the zoo
14 on a train
15 in a shop
16 on a shop door

23
(Suggestions)
1 at work, at the office, on the train
2 at a supermarket, at the grocer's, at the local shops, in town
3 in the cellar/garage, on the street, in the garden
4 at the post office, at the post box on the corner
5 at home, in the living-room, at my brother's
6 at a disco, in town
7 at a record shop, in the record department of a department store
8 in the shower, in the bathroom
9 at the bus-stop in X Street, on the corner, at the bus station
10 in a cafe/restaurant/pub, at the X club, at my house, at their houses

24
(Suggestions)
1 in the evenings, on hot days, on Saturday afternoons
2 in the morning, at breakfast, in the coffee-break
3 at about 10 pm
4 in the evening, at weekends, at work
5 on my birthday, on special occasions, on New Year's Eve, at (the) New Year
6 at about 12.30
7 at Christmas, on Christmas Eve/Day, on my birthday
8 at weekends, on their birthdays
9 on Saturdays, on weekdays, at lunch-time
10 in the evening, on Sunday morning, at 7 o'clock in the morning
11 at 6.30, at 8 o'clock
12 in summer, in July, at Christmas

25
1 are to 2 was to 3 is to 4 are to 5 were to
6 am to 7 were to 8 is to 9 are to 10 was to

26
(Suggestions)
1 I would choose a sports car because of its speed and appearance/because it goes fast and looks good.
I would choose a saloon car because of its size and comfort/because it's bigger and more comfortable than a sports car.
2 I would choose spaghetti and ice-cream because of their food value and good taste/because I like them.
I would choose fruit and yoghurt because of the low calories/the vitamins/because I'm on a diet/they are good for you.
3 I would choose a seaside holiday because of the sun and the swimming/because swimming is my favourite sport/because I like to relax in the sun.
I would choose a skiing holiday because of the snow and the mountains/because skiing's my favourite sport/because the fresh mountain air is good for you.
4 I would choose a big old house because of the big rooms/because I like old houses.
I would choose a small modern house because of the modern design and lower running costs/because a modern house is more convenient/because I don't need a big house.
5 I would choose a house in the country because of the fresh air and countryside/because I don't like noise and dirt.
I would choose a flat in the city because of the convenience of being close to shops and work/because I like city life.
6 I would choose a job in my own country because of the language/my family/because I am used to working conditions in my own country.
I would choose a job abroad because of the opportunities to learn a new language/the chance to earn more money/the experience and the challenge.

27
(Suggestions)
1 I usually clean my teeth before I have a shower.
2 I usually get dressed before I comb my hair.
3 I usually get dressed before I have breakfast.
4 I usually shave/put on my make-up before I comb my hair.
5 I usually have breakfast before I put on my shoes.
6 I usually make my bed before I have breakfast.
7 I usually read the newspaper before I have lunch.
8 I usually read the newspaper before I watch television.
9 I usually have supper before I watch television.
10 I usually get into bed before I put out the light.

28
1 before 2 in front of 3 in front of 4 before
5 before 6 in front of 7 in front of 8 before
9 in front of 10 before

29
1 a great president/man 2 a big/large car 3 a tall building 4 a great/big mistake 5 a great friend
6 a great/big country 7 a great idea 8 a tall tree
9 a great composer 10 a big/large flat

30
1 lend 2 borrow, lend 3 lend 4 borrow 5 lent
6 borrow 7 Lend 8 borrowing 9 lend, lent
10 borrow

31
They are both over 18.
They have both been abroad.
They both play a musical instrument.
They both hate examinations.
They both enjoy mathematics.
They both like dancing.
They can both drive a car.
They can both speak a foreign language.
They both have a girlfriend.
They can both play chess.

32
1 take 2 take 3 brings 4 take 5 take 6 bring
7 take, bring 8 bring/take 9 take 10 take

33
(Suggestions)
I can type very well.
I can drive a car quite well.
I can't use a pocket calculator at all.
I can take photographs quite well.
I can't play table tennis at all.
I can't use a sewing machine at all.
I can dance a bit.
I can paint quite well.
I can act a bit.
I can't play football at all.
I can cook very well.
I can't dive at all.
I can ride a bicycle quite well.
I can play the guitar a bit.
I can speak Japanese very well.

34
(Possible answers)
1 I think/don't think people/we will be able to live on another planet.
2 I think/don't think people/we will be able to live in space.
3 I think/don't think people/we will be able to live in towns on the sea-bed.
4 I think/don't think people/we will be able to build cities in the desert.
5 I think/don't think people/we will be able to go on holiday to the moon.
6 I think/don't think people/we will be able to fly private helicopters and small planes.
7 I think/don't think people/we will be able to grow food on the sea-bed.
8 I think/don't think people/we will be able to travel faster than light.

35
(Suggestions)
I could walk when I was two but I couldn't talk until I was three.
I could count to ten when I was five but I couldn't do geometry until I was eleven/went to secondary school.
I could say the alphabet when I was four but I couldn't read until I was six/started school.
I could write my name when I was five but I couldn't write a letter until I was eight.
I could swim when I was seven but I couldn't dive until I was ten.
I could play football when I was nine but I couldn't play chess until I was thirteen/a few weeks ago.
I could boil an egg when I was ten but I couldn't cook a meal until I was eighteen/left home.
I could ride a bicycle when I was six but I couldn't drive until I was seventeen/last year.

36
(Possible answers)
2 I think a dog can live up to 15 years. (Correct)
3 I think a rabbit can live up to 6 years. (Correct)
4 I think a horse can live up to 25 years. (Correct)
5 I think a mouse can live up to 2 years. (Correct)
6 I think a camel can live up to 40 years. (Correct)
7 I think a kangaroo can live up to 17 years. (Correct)
8 I think a tortoise can live up to 100 years. (Correct)
9 I think a fox can live up to 12 years. (Correct)
10 I think an elephant can live up to 70 years. (Correct)
11 I think a brown bear can live up to 24 years. (Correct)

37
(Possible answers)
It can't be suspect A because he has glasses/he's wearing glasses.
It can't be suspect B because he's short and fat/too short/too fat.
It can't be suspect C because he's got long hair/his hair's too long.
It can't be suspect D because he's got a moustache.
It can't be suspect E because he's too old/too short/too fat.
It can't be suspect F because he's got a beard.

38
(Possible answers)
1 Someone could have climbed through the window.
2 Someone could have stolen it.
3 There could have been a fire.
4 She could have had/caused an accident.
5 Someone could have taken it.
6 She could have broken her leg/ankle.
7 She could have caught a bad cold.
8 She could have drowned.
9 She could have fallen.
10 She could have been fined./She could have got a parking ticket.

39
(Possible answers)
1 Can I use your phone, please?
2 Can I borrow your pen, please?
3 Can I go now, please?
4 Can I try it on, please?
5 Can I give you a lift/ride?
6 Can I take your coat?
7 Can I help you to push?
8 Can I carry something for you?

40
(Possible answers)
She couldn't have male visitors at all/any male visitors.
She couldn't have parties.
She couldn't make a noise or play music after 9.30 pm.
She couldn't use the washing machine.
She could only use the telephone in an emergency.
She could only have one bath a week.
She couldn't keep food in her room.
She could only use the kitchen for making drinks, not for cooking food.

41
1 comes, come, go 2 go, came 3 go 4 come, come
5 come, come 6 went 7 came 8 goes 9 going, come

42
(Suggestions)
I'm thinner than he is.
She's darker than I am.
I'm fairer than he is.
I'm taller than she is.
He's younger than I am.
She's older than I am.
I'm more cheerful than she is.
He's cleverer than I am.
She's more practical than I am.
He's more polite than I am.
I'm more musical than he is.
He's stronger than I am.
I'm happier than he is.

43
The Astoria is the cheapest.
The Atlantis is the most expensive.
The Astoria is the farthest from the beach.
The Palm Beach is the farthest from the centre.
The Atlantis is the most luxurious.
The Palm Beach is the most modern.
The Palm Beach is the nearest to the beach.
The Astoria is the nearest to the centre.
The Palm Beach is the newest.
The Astoria is the oldest.
The Astoria is the smallest.

44
1 It's the driest country in the world.
2 It's the fastest passenger plane in the world.
3 It's the tallest tower in the world.
4 It's the longest river in the world.
5 It's the coldest place in the world.
6 It's the biggest/largest desert in the world.
7 It's the highest mountain in the world.
8 It's the city with the largest/biggest population in the world.
9 It's the wettest country in the world.
10 It's the busiest airport in the world.

45
(Possible answers)
1 It was a little cooler in Alexandria than in Cairo.
2 It was a little warmer in Glasgow than in Edinburgh.
3 It was no warmer in Malaga than in London.
4 It was very much cooler in Helsinki than in Stockholm.
5 It was a lot hotter in Riyadh than in Alexandria.
6 It was no hotter in Cairo than in Munich.
7 It was no warmer in Edinburgh than in Moscow.
8 It was much hotter in Luxor than in Alexandria.
9 It was a little cooler in Barcelona than in Madrid.
10 It was far cooler in Melbourne than in Sydney.

46
2 If he wasn't teaching, he would (he'd) be walking in the mountains.
3 If he wasn't having a hard day at the office, he'd be playing golf.
4 If she wasn't working late, she'd be watching a film on television.
5 If he wasn't mending his car, he'd be playing tennis.
6 If she wasn't doing the housework, she'd be lying in the sun.
7 If he wasn't practising the piano, he'd be rowing on the lake with his girlfriend.

47
(Suggestions)
1 If I left a restaurant with the wrong umbrella I would take it back immediately.
2 If a waiter in a restaurant overcharged me I would call him and ask him to check the bill.
3 If I missed the last bus home I would try to get a taxi.
4 If I missed my station on the train I would get off at the next station and wait for the next train back.
5 If I got lost in a big city I would ask the way or I would buy a street map.
6 If someone stole my wallet I would report it to the police.
7 If I lost my passport I would inform the passport office/ the consulate and apply for a new one.
8 If a stranger asked me for a lift at night I would ask him a lot of questions/I would refuse/I would probably help him.
9 If someone offered me a briefcase full of money I would tell him or her to take it to the police/I would take it and say 'Thank you!'.
10 If I got stuck in a lift I would push the alarm button.

48
1 We all know that English is a difficult language to learn well.
2 As you can see, I'm very busy.
3 The sun is shining, but it isn't very warm.
4 Although he's very rich, he doesn't waste money.
5 Because I hadn't saved enough money, I couldn't buy the car.
6 I liked him, so I trusted him.
7 Because I didn't trust him, I didn't help him.
8 You will understand that I can't pay the whole sum at once.
9 Although she's very busy, she's always willing to help.
10 He's very fat, but he doesn't eat much.

49
2 She looks lonely. 3 It tastes delicious. 4 It sounds terrible. 5 It feels soft. 6 They smell beautiful. 7 It sounds delightful. 8 It smells burnt. 9 He feels hot. 10 It looks expensive. 11 It tastes bitter. 12 He looks cold. 13 She looks sad.

50
(Suggestions)
1 People in my country usually have cereal/eggs/bread or toast/coffee etc.
2 I usually have a bowl of cornflakes/an egg/a slice of bread/a cup of coffee etc.

51
British English:
Pisces, from February the twentieth to March the twentieth/ from the twentieth of February to the twentieth of March.
Aries, from March the twenty-first to April the twentieth/from the twenty-first of March to the twentieth of April.
Taurus, from April the twenty-first to May the twenty-second/ from the twenty-first of April to the twenty-second of May.
Gemini, from May the twenty-third to June the twenty-first/ from the twenty-third of May to the twenty-first of June.
Cancer, from June the twenty-second to July the twenty-second/from the twenty-second of June to the twenty-second of July.
Leo, from July the twenty-third to August the twenty-second/ from the twenty-third of July to the twenty-second of August.
Virgo, from August the twenty-third to September the twenty-second/from the twenty-third of August to the twenty-second of September.

Libra, from September the twenty-third to October the twenty-second/from the twenty-third of September to the twenty-second of October.
Scorpio, from October the twenty-third to November the twenty-first/from the twenty-third of October to the twenty-first of November.
Saggitarius, from November the twenty-second to December the twenty-second/from the twenty-second of November to the twenty-second of December.
Capricorn, from December the twenty-third to January the twentieth/from the twenty-third of December to the twentieth of January.
American English:
Pisces, from February twentieth to March twentieth, etc.

52
1 In 1964 (nineteen sixty-four), the Olympic Games were held in Tokyo.
2 In 1968 (nineteen sixty-eight), the Olympic Games were held in Mexico City.
3 In 1972 (nineteen seventy-two), the Olympic Games were held in Munich.
4 In 1976 (nineteen seventy-six), the Olympic Games were held in Montreal.
5 In 1980 (nineteen eighty), the Olympic Games were held in Moscow.
6 In 1984 (nineteen eighty-four), the Olympic Games were held in Los Angeles.

53
(Suggestions)

I don't drink strong coffee.	I don't like snakes.
I don't stay out late at night.	I don't travel a lot.
I don't go to bed early.	I don't enjoy walking.
I don't smoke.	I can't ski.
I don't believe in horoscopes.	I don't like horror films.
I don't like music.	I don't listen to jazz.
I can't write shorthand.	I can't play the trumpet.
I can't speak Chinese.	I don't watch much television.
I can't drive a car.	I don't enjoy washing up.

54
(Suggestions)
I do a lot of walking in summer. I don't do much cleaning at the weekends. I do my shopping on Saturdays.

55
do homework, a favour, housework, business, the washing-up, one's best, one's duty, the shopping, the cooking, military service.
make a mistake, a journey, the beds, a cake, bread, arrangements, a decision, an excuse, a model plane, a phone call.

56
1 for 2 during 3 for 4 for 5 during 6 for 7 During 8 during 9 for 10 during

57
1 during 2 during 3 during 4 in, in 5 during 6 during 7 during/in 8 during 9 during/in 10 during/in

58
(Suggestions)
Good friends trust each other/one another.
Good friends help each other/one another.
Good friends enjoy each other's/one another's company.
Good friends can rely on each other/one another, etc.

59

1 nobody else 2 somebody else's 3 much else/
anything else 4 Everybody else 5 Where else
6 everything else/what else 7 everywhere else
8 anything else, nothing else 9 Who else 10 what else

60

1c It was to the airport that John drove Diana on Sunday.
1d It was on Sunday that John drove Diana to the airport.
2a It was Jill that phoned her mother from Paris last week.
2b It was her mother that Jill phoned from Paris last week.
2c It was from Paris that Jill phoned her mother last week.
2d It was last week that Jill phoned her mother from Paris.
3a It was Mrs Brown that met Sally in the supermarket
   yesterday.
3b It was Sally that Mrs Brown met in the supermarket
   yesterday.
3c It was in the supermarket that Mrs Brown met Sally
   yesterday.
3d It was yesterday that Mrs Brown met Sally in the
   supermarket.

61

(Suggestions)
I enjoy/don't enjoy taking photographs, dancing, doing
housework, riding motorbikes, repairing my car, travelling by
bus, smoking a pipe, lying in the bath, sitting in the sun,
doing homework, playing tennis, watching television, flying,
cycling, washing the car.

62

1 lucky enough 2 strong enough 3 hard enough
4 fast enough 5 deep enough 6 tall/big enough
7 loud(ly) enough 8 warm enough 9 well enough
10 fluently enough

63

He hasn't got enough Coca Cola.
He hasn't got enough beer.
He's got enough wine.
He hasn't got enough sausage rolls.
He hasn't got enough cheese biscuits.
He's got enough packets of crisps.
He's got enough chocolate biscuits.
He hasn't got enough glasses.
He's got enough plates.
He hasn't got enough chairs.

64

(Suggestions)
He/She is old enough to ride a motor-bike. He/She isn't old
enough to be sent to prison, etc.

65

1 Even though I didn't work very hard for the exam, I passed.
2 Even though I don't speak Greek, I made a lot of friends
   in Athens.
3 Even though Mr Collins doesn't earn much, he's always
   well dressed.
4 Even though Sylvia hasn't got many friends, she's always
   out.
5 Even though Robert hasn't had a good education, he's
   got a good job.
6 Even though Jill Stewart has four children, her house is
   always clean and tidy.
7 Even though Mrs Poole doesn't eat much, she puts on
   weight.
8 Even though Terry has stopped smoking, he still has a
   cough.
9 Even though the sun didn't shine all day, it was very warm.
10 Even though I sat in the shade all day, I got a sun-tan.

66

(Suggestions)
Do you ever travel abroad for your company? Do you ever
watch horror films? Have you ever smoked? Have you ever
read an Agatha Christie novel? etc.

67

(Possible answers)
1 They're all tools except the key.
2 They all need electricity except the candle.
3 They're all sharp except the paintbrush.
4 They're all fruits except the mushroom.
5 You smoke them all except the ash-tray.
6 Except for the bucket, we drink from them all.
7 Except for the ring, they are all made of wood.
8 Except for the foot, they are all parts of your face.
9 Except for the alarm clock, they are all musical instruments.
10 Except for the goose, they all have four legs.

68

(Possible answers)
2 What beautiful flowers! How lovely those flowers are!
3 What terrible weather! How dark and cold it looks outside!
4 How delicious it looks!
5 What a lot of money!
6 What a fat man!
7 How beautifully she sings What a lovely voice she has!
8 What dirty hands you've/he's got!
9 What a cold room! How cold it is in here!

69

A dictionary explains the meanings of words to you.
A grammar explains language rules to you.
Politicians explain their policies to you.
Teachers explain school subjects to you.
Scientists explain the natural world to you.
Meteorologists explain the weather to you.
A lawyer explains the law to you.
A doctor explains your illnesses to you.
A journalist explains the news to you.
Religion explains the meaning of life to you.
A psychologist explains human behaviour to you.

70

1 quite 2 rather 3 pretty/rather 4 quite
5 fairly/quite 6 rather/pretty 7 rather 8 fairly
9 quite/rather 10 rather/pretty

71

1 far 2 a long way 3 far 4 far 5 a long way 6 far
7 a long way 8 far 9 far 10 far

72

1 farther/further 2 further 3 further 4 farther/further
5 farther/further 6 further 7 further 8 farther/further
9 further 10 further

73

1 (a) few 2 little 3 little 4 a few 5 little 6 a few
7 few 8 few 9 little

74

There's a little sugar, rice, spaghetti, milk, cheese, butter,
bread, jam, coffee, mineral water left, and there are a few
tomatoes, carrots, potatoes, peas, eggs and biscuits.

75
1 You should eat less salt, fewer fried foods and more fresh vegetables.
2 You should eat more raw salads and fewer canned foods.
3 You should eat less sugar, fewer sweet foods and more honey.
4 You should eat more fish, less meat and fewer eggs.
5 You should eat more vegetable oils and less butter.
6 You should eat less white bread and more wholemeal bread.
7 You should eat less cream, more natural yoghurt and fewer puddings.
8 You should drink less coffee, more caffeine-free drinks and fewer cola-drinks.
9 You should drink less alcohol and more fresh natural fruit juices.
10 You should eat fewer salted nuts and more soya beans.

76
There was less pollution, industry, crime, traffic, unemployment, danger of world war, inflation. There were fewer factories, motorways, road deaths, nuclear weapons, people out of work, millionaires, terrorists.

77
(Possible answers)
1 I'd go to the post office for stamps.
2 I'd go to the library for books or records.
3 I'd go to the doctor's for an examination or a prescription.
4 I'd go to the newsagent's for a newspaper or magazine.
5 I'd go to a restaurant for a meal.
6 I'd go to the bank for some money.
7 I'd go to the baker's for bread or cakes.
8 I'd go to the supermarket for food.
9 I'd go to the travel agent's for holiday brochures and information.
10 I'd go to the chemist's for tablets and medicine.

78
(Possible answers)
1 That's a ruler. We use it for measuring things.
2 That's a hammer. We use it for knocking nails into wood.
3 That's a screwdriver. We use it for putting in screws.
4 Those are scissors. We use them for cutting things.
5 Those are binoculars. We use them for looking at things in the distance.
6 That's a hair-dryer. We use it for drying hair.
7 That's an iron. We use it for ironing clothes.
8 That's a sewing machine. We use it for making clothes.
9 That's a camera. We use it for taking photographs.
10 That's a vacuum cleaner. We use it for cleaning carpets.
11 Those are keys. We use them for locking and unlocking things.
12 That's a lawn-mower. We use it for mowing the lawn.

79
(Suggestions)
1 Yes, it's usual for pupils to attend school until they are 16 or older.
2 Yes, it's common for people to own a house or flat.
3 No, it's uncommon for people to have several children.
4 Yes, it's common for women to have a driving licence.
5 No, it's uncommon for old people to live with their children.
6 No, it's rare for women to join the armed forces.
7 No, it's unusual for unmarried couples to live together.
8 Yes, it's usual for people to join a political party or trade union.
9 No, it's rare for great numbers of people to be unemployed.
10 Yes, it's normal for people to learn English at school.

80
1 It's also quite common for learners to take their driving test three times.
2 It's usual for people to pass the test the second time.
3 It's important for all beginners to take some lessons with a driving instructor.
4 It's usual for the driving instructor to point out mistakes.
5 It's essential for learner drivers to keep their eyes on the road, not on the signs.
6 It's important for nervous drivers to try to keep calm.
7 It's quite essential for the learner to feel confident and not panic.
8 It's quite normal for people to feel very nervous on the day of the test.
9 It's usual for examiners to be quite strict.
10 It's rare for a nervous driver to pass the test the first time.

81
1 since 1973 2 for 5 years 3 for 6 years 4 since 1975 5 for 4 years 6 since 1980 7 since 1983 8 for 3 years 9 for 1 year 10 for 9 months

82
(Suggestions)
1 I've lived here since 19. ./for . . . years.
2 My parents have lived in our town for many years/since they were born.
3 We've been living in our present house/flat for just three months/since Christmas last year.
4 I've been able to ride a bicycle for twenty years/since I was four. I've been able to drive a car since my seventeenth birthday.
5 I've had a bicycle since my sixth birthday. I've had a car for about five years now.
6 I've known my best friend for over twenty years/since we were children.
7 I've known my English teacher for two years/since the beginning of this year.
8 I've been able to swim for . . . years/since I was . . . .
9 I've been engaged/married for . . . years/months/since 19 . . .
10 I've had my present job for . . . years/months/since last year.

83
(Suggestions)
3 My brother's going to a football match on Saturday.
4 My wife and I are visiting an aunt and uncle on Sunday.
5 I'm going camping on my next holiday.

84
(Possible answers)
2 He's going to jump.
3 The doctor's going to give him an injection.
4 They're going to race.
5 She's going to drop the books.
6 He's going to dive into the water.
7 The plane's going to land.
8 He's going to make a phone call.
9 They're going to paint the house.
10 She's going to fall off.

85
(Possible answers)
I'm going to/not going to make a telephone call, learn English vocabulary, read a book, visit a friend, listen to records, play cards, write a letter, cook supper/a meal, clean my room, go to bed early, have a meal in a restaurant.

86

(Suggestions)

Working conditions will be much better. Everybody will have more leisure time. There won't be enough oil. etc.

87

(Suggestions)

How many children will I have? Will I have a long life? Who will I marry? Will I be successful in my job? etc.

88

. . . he arrives at King's Cross Station, London at 17.49. He stays overnight in London at the Victoria Hotel. He departs from London, Victoria Station, at 8.00 and arrives in Dover at 9.25. He crosses to Ostend by Jetfoil at 10.00 and arrives at 11.40. He leaves Ostend by train at 12.15 and arrives in Frankfurt at 19.10.

89

(Possible answers)

By the year 2000, Tokyo will have gone down to third position.
By the year 2000, São Paulo will have moved up to second position/the population of São Paulo will have increased from 12.8 million to 24 million.
By the year 2000, Shanghai will have gone down to eighth position/the population of Shanghai will have increased from 11.8 million to 13.5 million.
By the year 2000, Buenos Aires will have gone down to eleventh position/the population of Buenos Aires will have increased from 10.1 million to 13.2 million.
By the year 2000, Calcutta will have moved up to fourth position/the population of Calcutta will have increased from 9.5 million to 16.6 million.
By the year 2000, Rio de Janeiro will have moved up to ninth position/the population of Rio de Janeiro will have increased from 9.2 million to 13.3 million.
By the year 2000, Bombay will have moved up to fifth position.
By the year 2000, Seoul will have moved up to seventh position.

90

1 Terry will have saved £150 in 3 months' time.
2 Janet will have saved £48 in 6 weeks' time.
3 Ted will have saved £260 in 4 months' time.
4 Maria will have saved £600 in 6 months' time.
5 Barry won't have saved anything in a month's time.
6 Jeff will have saved £60 in 10 weeks' time.
7 Helen will have saved £210 in 3 months' time.
8 Celia won't have saved any money in a month's time.
9 Betty will have saved £100 in 10 weeks' time.
10 John won't have saved anything in 10 weeks' time.

91

1 At 8.00 tomorrow he'll be sitting on the plane to Paris/he'll be flying to Paris.
2 At 8.55 tomorrow he'll be landing in Paris.
3 At 9.20 tomorrow he'll be meeting M. Chevalier.
4 At 9.30 tomorrow he'll be driving to company headquarters.
5 At 10.15 tomorrow he'll be having a meeting with the Board of Directors.
6 At 12.15 tomorrow he'll be having lunch with Max Peters.
7 At 14.15 tomorrow he'll be giving a lecture.
8 At 15.00 tomorrow he'll be phoning New York.
9 At 15.45 tomorrow he'll be having a meeting with Bill Morris.
10 At 16.30 tomorrow he'll be leaving for the airport.
11 At 18.00 tomorrow his flight home will be leaving/he'll be leaving for home/he'll be taking off.
12 At 18.30 tomorrow he'll be flying home/he'll be sitting on the plane going home.

92

1 answer 2 bought 3 caught 4 take 5 arrive 6 receive/tune in to 7 understand 8 catch, write down/note 9 turns/becomes/goes 10 move/fit 11 order 12 received

93

2 Japan 3 Kenya 4 Egypt 5 Australia 6 London/England 7 Holland 8 New York/America 9 Pisa/Italy 10 Paris/France 11 Spain 12 India.

94

1 It goes soft. 2 It goes dry/hard. 3 It goes hard. 4 It goes bad. 5 It goes soft. 6 It goes flat. 7 It goes sour. 8 It goes stale/dry. 9 It goes limp.

95

(Suggestions)

I sometimes/never/often/occasionally go . . . 2 riding 3 running 4 skiing 5 water-skiing 6 sailing 7 wind-surfing 8 hiking/walking 9 mountain climbing 10 snorkeling 11 dancing 12 fishing 13 swimming 14 rifle shooting

96

(Possible answers)

1 You'd better go to bed early.
2 You'd better get/have it cut.
3 You'd better look for it.
4 You'd better hurry.
5 You'd better not drink it.
6 You'd better throw it away/not eat it.
7 You'd better stay in bed.
8 You'd better take it.
9 You'd better wash/clean it.
10 You'd better not lose it/put it in a safe place.

97

1 hardly 2 hard 3 hardly 4 hardly 5 hard 6 hard 7 hardly 8 hard 9 hardly 10 hard

98

1 Thailand has a king. 2 Japan has an emperor. 3 Norway and Sweden have a king. 4 Oman has a sultan. 5 Denmark and Holland have a queen. 6 Belgium has a king. 7 Morocco has a king. 8 Brunei has a sultan. 9 Spain has a king. 10 Saudi Arabia and Jordan have a king.

99

(Suggestions)

My sister's got a scooter. We haven't got a parrot. My parents have got a house. My uncle's got a caravan. I've got a watch. We haven't got a video-recorder. My father's got some classical records. We've all got tennis rackets. We've got a telephone. We haven't got a piano. My brother's got a football. My parents have got a car. I've got a tent. We haven't got a dog. We've each got a radio. My brother's got a bicycle. We haven't got a micro-wave. We've got a dishwasher. We've all got a pair of glasses. We've got two televisions. My mother's got a camera. My father's got a briefcase.

100
(Possible answers)

2 They have breakfast at 8 o'clock./At 8 o'clock they have breakfast.
3 Janet has coffee at the office at 10 o'clock./At 10 o'clock Janet. . .
4 Frank has lunch in the canteen at 12.30./At 12.30 Frank. . .
5 Frank has a chat with his colleagues after lunch./After lunch Frank. . .
6 They have tea at 3 o'clock./At 3 o'clock they. . .
7 Frank has a beer with his friends after work./After work. . .
8 In the evening, they sometimes have a glass of wine./They sometimes have. . .
9 In the evening, Janet usually has a bath./Janet usually has. . .
10 At the weekend, they often have a game of tennis./They often have. . .
11 At the weekend, they sometimes have a meal at/in a restaurant./They sometimes have. . .

101

2 He's having his eyes tested.
3 They're having a house built.
4 She's having a dress made.
5 He's having his car washed.
6 She's having her fortune told.
7 He's having his portrait painted.
8 She's having her hands manicured.
9 They're having their house painted.
10 He's having a suit made.
11 She's having her bicycle repaired.

102
(Suggestions)

1 No, I've never had a tooth extracted.
2 No, I've never had my heart examined.
3 Yes, I've had my hearing tested twice.
4 Yes, I've had my blood pressure checked several times.
5 Yes, I've had a blood sample taken three or four times.
6 Yes, I've had my lungs X-rayed twice.

103
(Suggestions)

On Tuesday, I've got to take the car to be serviced.
On Wednesday, I've got to go to the doctor's.
On Thursday, I've got to go to Rome with my boss.

104
(Suggestions)

1 You have to entertain a lot in the evenings. You have to travel quite a lot.
2 You have to spend most of your time underground. You have to work shifts.
3 You have to work at a conveyor belt. You have to work shifts.
4 You have to train several hours a day. You have to end your career at an early age.
5 You have to stand most of the time. You sometimes have to deal with difficult customers.
6 You have to look your best all the time. You have to smile and laugh even when you don't feel like it. You have to wear a lot of make-up.
7 You have to sit at a desk for hours. You have to work regular office-hours.
8 You have to work outside in all kinds of weather. You have to start work very early.
9 You have to stand all the time. You sometimes have to deal ̣ difficult customers. You have to work on Saturdays.
     ̣ walk about a lot. You have to work at nights.

105

1 hear 2 hear 3 listening to 4 heard 5 listen
6 listening to 7 hear 8 hear 9 listens to
10 listened 11 heard 12 hear 13 listening

106

1 left home 2 go home 3 come home 4 arrive home
5 drive home 6 brought home 7 get home 8 ran home 9 walk home 10 takes home

107
(Possible answers)

1 . . .you get cold feet/. . .you catch a cold.
2 . . .you get out of breath.
3 . . .you get drunk/you feel terrible.
4 . . .you get wet.
5 . . .you are always short of money.
6 If you eat too much/If you don't get enough exercise. . .
7 If you don't eat enough/If you go on a strict diet. . .
8 If you read for a long time/If you read in a bad light. . .
9 If you smoke too many cigarettes. . .
10 If you eat too many sweet things/If you don't look after your teeth properly. . .

108
(Suggestions)

1 If I won £10, I would (I'd) go out for a meal.
2 If I won £100, I would buy myself something nice.
3 If I won £1000, I would put it in the bank.
4 If I won £10,000, I would go on a world trip.
5 If I won £100,000, I'd buy a house.
6 If I won £1,000,000, I'd give up work and live on a Greek island.

109

1 If you hired a Ford Sierra for a weekend it would cost £53.
2 If you hired a BL Metro for 3 days it would cost £61.50
3 If you hired a BMW 316 for 2 weeks it would cost £398.
4 If you hired a Ford Fiesta for 5 days it would cost £102.50
5 If you hired a BL Montego for a week it would cost £140.
6 If you hired a Ford Orion for 2 weeks it would cost £280.
7 If you hired a Vauxhall Nova for a weekend it would cost £42.
8 If you hired a Ford Escort for 4 days it would cost £88.
9 If you hired a BL Maestro for 2 weeks it would cost £238.
10 If you hired a Vauxhall Cavalier for 3 weeks it would cost £420.

110
(Possible answers)

1 If she hadn't forgotten to lock the car, the camera wouldn't have got stolen.
2 If he hadn't left his wallet in a restaurant, it wouldn't have disappeared.
3 If she hadn't left her watch lying about, it wouldn't have got broken.
4 If he had locked the door of his flat, thieves wouldn't have broken in.
5 If she hadn't knocked her glasses off the table, they wouldn't have broken.
6 If she had put her name on her suitcase, someone wouldn't have taken it by mistake.
7 If he hadn't parked his car without lights, another car wouldn't have run into it.
8 If he had looked after his bicycle, it wouldn't have gone rusty.
9 If she hadn't left her parcels on a bus, no one would have taken them.
10 If he had kept his passport in a safe place, it wouldn't have got lost.

111

(Possible answers)
It would have cost less if he had flown from Gatwick.
It would have cost less if he had gone in May.
It would have been cheaper if he had stayed at the Palace Hotel.
It would have been cheaper if he hadn't booked a single room.
It would have cost less if he hadn't booked full board.

112

(Suggestions)
1 If you went to London, you could see Buckingham Palace/practise your English.
2 If you went to Scotland, you could visit Edinburgh and see Loch Ness.
3 If you went to New York, you could see the Statue of Liberty/practise speaking English.
4 If you went to Paris, you could go up the Eiffel Tower/practise French.
5 If you went to Kenya, you could see the animals in the game reserves/go on safari.
6 If you went to India, you could visit the Taj Mahal.
7 If you went to Mexico, you could see Acapulco and practise Spanish.
8 If you went to Egypt, you could visit the pyramids at Gizeh.
9 If you went to Switzerland, you could go skiing/enjoy the good cheese and chocolate.
10 If you went to Italy, you could visit Rome and Florence/see some beautiful works of art.

113

1 She often thinks to herself, 'If only I could speak a foreign language.'
2 He often thinks to himself, 'If only I hadn't sold my old car.'
3 She often thinks to herself, 'If only I wasn't afraid of water.'
4 He often thinks to himself, 'If only I hadn't failed my driving test.'
5 He often thinks to himself, 'If only I had taken A-Level English at school.'
6 She often thinks to herself, 'If only I hadn't left school at 16.'
7 She often thinks to herself, 'If only I could play a musical instrument.'
8 He often thinks to himself, 'If only I had gone to America when I had the chance.'
9 He often thinks to himself, 'If only I played tennis.'
10 He often thinks to himself, 'If only I was a good businessman.'

114

(Suggestions)
Don't arrive late! Ask lots of intelligent questions! Write down a list of things you want to know, etc.

115

1 find, stop, Don't try, Move, give   2 Stand, Don't stand
3 Look, listen   4 let, Look   5 walk, don't cross,
Remember, walk, don't run   6 Keep

116

1 Do exercise   2 Don't let   3 Do keep   4 Don't leave
5 Do see   6 Don't let   7 Do feed   8 Don't keep
9 Do have   10 Don't let

117

(Suggestions)
1 in case it gets cold.
2 in case you can't buy anything on the way.
3 in case you get really hungry.
4 in case it starts to rain heavily.

5 in case you get lost.
6 in case you lose your direction.
7 in case the sun's very bright.
8 in case you get blisters on your feet.
9 in case you need to buy anything.
10 in case anything happens.

118

1 in spite of the icy roads.
2 in spite of the dangerous roads.
3 in spite of his inexperience.
4 in spite of the fog.
5 in spite of the bad weather forecast.
6 in spite of the heavy snow.
7 in spite of his illness.
8 in spite of the doctor's warning.
9 in spite of the high price.
10 in spite of my advice.

119

(Possible answers)
Number three wants you to use the telephone. Number four wants you to rent a car. Number five wants people to learn French. Number six wants you to buy a second-hand car. Number seven wants people to book cheap flights. Number eight wants you to buy a retirement home. Number nine wants people to buy Greek oranges. Number ten wants people to buy property in Switzerland. Number eleven wants you to hire a bicycle. Number twelve wants people to donate money to charity/send donations.

120

(Possible answers)
It tells you to enter the water slowly and carefully.
It warns you never to be caught off your guard.
It advises you never to swim alone.
It tells you always to have someone you can call to.
It warns you to dive beneath breaking waves before they reach you.
It warns you not to stand in the path of a large wave.
It tells you not to swim over a large wave or turn your back against it.
It advises you to avoid beaches with rocky coasts.
It tells you to stay clear of areas with surfers.
It advises you to look out for runaway surfboards that wash in with the waves.

121

(Suggestions)
I would tell/show them where to stay, how to make our national dish, what to see in our area, where to find information, how to say a few words in our language, etc.

122

(Possible answers)
2 I'd go to a car rental agency to hire a car.
3 I'd go to an optician's to have my eyes tested.
4 I'd go to a box office to book tickets for the theatre or for a concert.
5 I'd go to a filling station to buy petrol.
6 I'd go to a Citizen's Advice Bureau to find out what to do about noisy neighbours.
7 I'd go to a jeweller's to buy jewellery or a watch.
8 I'd go to an estate agent's to enquire about buying or selling a house or flat.
9 I'd go to a chemist's to buy tablets and medicine.
10 I'd go to an embassy to apply for a visa/work permit.
11 I'd go to an employment agency to look for a job.

123

(Possible answers)
1 Some people need an alarm clock to wake them in the mornings.
2 Some people need a walking stick to help them to walk better.
3 Some people need glasses to help them to see better.
4 Some people need a hearing aid to help them to hear better.
5 Some people use hair dye to change the colour of their hair.
6 Some people use make-up to improve their appearance.
7 Some people use perfume/aftershave to make themselves smell pleasant to others.
8 Some people use artificial sweeteners to replace sugar and reduce calories.
9 Some people need medicine and tablets to make them better when they are ill.
10 Some people need a safe to keep valuable things in.

124

(Suggestions)
1 Businessmen and -women need English in order to do business with foreign companies.
2 Secretaries need English in order to be able to work for international companies.
3 Scientists need English in order to read about research and developments in other countries.
4 Engineers need English in order to be able to work on international projects.
5 Pilots need English in order to communicate by radio with all countries.
6 Housewives want to learn English in order to be able to talk to foreigners in everyday situations, on holiday, or to help their children with English homework.
7 Journalists need English in order to interview foreigners and to read the international press.
8 People in the travel business need English in order to be able to give information to foreign tourists and to do business with international partners.

125

(Suggestions)
collecting stamps, gardening, building model aeroplanes, etc.

126

(Suggestions)
2 I dislike wasting time, making excuses, sewing on buttons.
3 I enjoy chatting on the telephone, looking after children.
4 I often feel like wasting time, sleeping late.
5 I would like to give up smoking.
6 I don't mind repairing things, cooking, getting up early.
7 I often try to put off making excuses, writing thank-you letters.
8 I don't like to risk taking on responsibility, sleeping late.
9 I can't stand arguing about money, watching horror films, wasting time.

127

(Possible answers)
The plants need watering.
The floor needs cleaning.
The windows need washing.
The waste-paper basket needs emptying.
The lamp needs fixing.
The book shelf needs repairing.
The dishes need washing.
The ashtray needs emptying.
The papers need tidying.
The clothes need hanging up.

128

(Suggestions)
By selling something that everybody wants to buy. By becoming a film star. By writing a best-seller.

129

1 Remember to close the windows.
2 Don't forget to cancel the newspapers.
3 Remember to turn off the water and electricity.
4 Don't forget to give your holiday address to the neighbours.
5 Remember to ask the post office to forward your mail.
6 He couldn't remember closing the windows.
7 He couldn't remember cancelling the newspapers.
8 He couldn't remember turning off the water and electricity.
9 He couldn't remember giving his holiday address to the neighbours.
10 He couldn't remember asking the post office to forward his mail.

130

awoke, awoken; become, became; break, broken; brought, brought; caught, caught; choose, chose; fall, fell; feel, felt; grew, grown; keep, kept; knew, known; lay, laid; leave, left; lie, lay; ride, ridden; rise, rose; shine, shone; spend, spent; stole, stolen; teach, taught; wear, wore.

131

(Possible answers)
1 It's time you had/got it cut.
2 It's time you lost weight/went on a diet.
3 It's time you cut them.
4 It's time you cleaned them.
5 It's time you put on a clean one.
6 It's time you washed them/put on clean ones.
7 It's time you tidied it up.
8 It's time you looked after it/took it to a garage.
9 It's time you paid me back.
10 It's time you gave it back to me.

132

(Possible answers)

2 Let's go swimming.	8 Let's book a holiday.
3 Let's go to the museum.	9 Let's go to the cinema/go to see a film.
4 Let's go to a concert.	
5 Let's have a coffee.	10 Let's take the underground/tube.
6 Let's take a taxi.	
7 Let's go for a meal.	11 Let's watch television.

133

1 seen   2 watch   3 see   4 see   5 looked at
6 watches   7 look   8 saw   9 look at   10 watched, look

134

(Suggestions)
I may buy a new car. I may get engaged. I may get a job abroad.

135

(Possible answers)
1 She's worried that she might not get the job.
2 He's worried that he might lose his job.
3 She's worried that it might not suit her.
4 He's worried he might have to sell it.
5 She's worried that she might not pass it.
6 He's worried that he won't get on with her.

7 She's worried that he might leave her.
8 She's worried that she might not finish it in time.
9 He's woried that he might not get it.
10 He's worried that she might end their friendship.

136
(Possible answers)
1 May I use your telephone, please?
2 May I smoke?
3 May I have some writing paper and an envelope, please?
4 May I turn on the heating in my room, please?
5 May I have a shower now, please?
6 May I play the records in my room?
7 May I have the salt, please?
8 May I look at the newspapers, please?
9 May I watch the news on TV, please?
10 May I have/take a walk round the garden?

137
(Suggestions)
I eat a lot of eggs. I don't eat much meat. I drink lots of coffee. I don't drink much wine. I don't eat much cake. I eat a lot of fruit. I don't eat many sweets. I eat a lot of cheese.

138
(Possible answers)
1 I must take it to be repaired.   6 I must stop smoking.
2 I must wash it.   7 I must pay them.
3 I must go to the doctor's.   8 I must post them immediately.
4 I must lose weight.   9 I must have it cut.
5 I must go to the dentist's.   10 I must tidy it (up).

139
You mustn't pick mushrooms.
You mustn't collect butterflies or snails.
You mustn't catch fish.
You mustn't collect stones or rocks.
You mustn't play radios.
You mustn't make/light fires.
You mustn't put up tents.
You mustn't drop litter.
You mustn't drive a car or motorbike.

140
(Possible answers)
1 It can't belong to Liz or the children. It must belong to Jim or Henry.
2 It can't belong to the men or the children. It must belong to Liz.
3 It can't belong to Liz or the children. It must belong to Jim or Henry.
4 They can't belong to the men or the children. They must belong to Liz.
5 It can't belong to the children. It must belong to Liz or the men.
6 They can't belong to Liz or the men. They must belong to Peter or Jenny.
7 It can't belong to Liz or the children. It must belong to Jim or Henry.
8 It can't belong to Liz or the men. It must belong to the children.
9 It can't belong to the children or the men. It must belong to Liz.
10 It can't belong to Liz or the men. It must belong to Peter or Jenny.

141
(Possible answers)
1 He must have bought a new one.
2 She must have gone out.
3 She can't have eaten them all.
4 He must have lost them.
5 Jane must have told her.
6 He can't have heard me.
7 There must have been an accident.
8 Where can she have put them?
9 Someone must have stolen it.
10 He can't have got home yet.

142
1 Spain   2 Norway   3 Ivory Coast   4 Algeria   5 Italy
6 Greece   7 Switzerland   8 East Germany   9 Japan
10 Denmark

143
1 Spanish   2 English   3 German   4 French, Flemish
5 Portuguese   6 English, French   7 Danish   8 Dutch
9 Arabic   10 Greek   11 Japanese   12 French
13 German, French, Italian, Romansch   14 Thai
15 Turkish   16 Welsh, English

144
2 She's an Italian.   3 He's an American.   4 She's a Greek.   5 He's a Russian.   6 She's an American.   7 He's Chinese.   8 He's a German.   9 He's a Pole.   10 He's a Czech.   11 She's an Englishwoman.

145
(Possible answers)
The Chinese are famous for their food and their silk.
The French make famous perfumes, wines and cognac.
The Germans make good cars and good beer. The Americans . . . The Greeks . . . The Dutch . . . The Italians . . . The Japanese . . . The Russians . . . The Scots . . . The Swiss . . . The Thais . . .

146
the British pound, the French franc, the Greek drachma, the Indian rupee, the Italian lira, the Japanese yen, the Mexican peso, the Spanish peseta, the Swedish krona, the American dollar

147
1 needn't   2 needn't have   3 need   4 Do we need?
5 needn't   6 needn't have   7 needn't   8 need
9 needn't   10 didn't need   11 needn't   12 don't need/didn't need

148
1 Neither is the Woodland Hotel.
2 Neither has the Woodland Hotel.
3 Neither does the Riverside Hotel.
4 Neither are the Riverside Hotel and the Woodland Hotel.
5 Neither have the Bridge Hotel and the Woodland Hotel.
6 Neither do the Bridge Hotel and the Riverside Hotel.
7 Neither has the Bridge Hotel.
8 Neither has the Bridge Hotel.
9 Neither have the Riverside Hotel and the Woodland Hotel.
10 Neither does the Bridge Hotel.

149

Neither Elena nor Pierre went to Oxford Street.
Neither Pablos nor Kirsten went to 10 Downing Street.
Neither José nor Pierre went to Westminster Abbey.
Neither Elena nor Kirsten went to St. Paul's Cathedral.
Neither Ali nor Pablos went to the Houses of Parliament.
Neither Ali nor José went to the British Museum.
Neither Pierre nor Yasuko went to the Tower of London.
Neither Elena nor José went to the Tate Gallery.
Neither Kirsten nor Yasuko went to a pub.
Neither José nor Pierre went to Speakers' Corner.

150

1 next   2 nearest   3 nearest, next   4 nearest, next
5 nearest, next   6 next   7 next   8 nearest   9 next

151

1 None   2 neither   3 No   4 None   5 None   6 no
7 no   8 Neither   9 No   10 No, no

152

1 not   2 no   3 No   4 not   5 No   6 No   7 not
8 Not   9 No   10 no

153

a seven tenths   b one sixth   c five eighths   d three
quarters   e two thirds   f three fifths

154

1 one two three
2 oh one, two four six, eight oh four three
3 nine nine nine
4 one nine two
5 oh one, two four six, eight oh nine one
6 oh one, two four six, eight oh two oh
7 a hundred (or one hundred)
8 oh one, two four six, eight oh four one
9 oh one, two four six, eight oh three oh
10 oh one, two four six, eight oh double three

155

1 Elizabeth the Second   2 George the Sixth   3 Charles
the Third   4 Elizabeth the First   5 Henry the Eighth
6 Charles the First

156

1 on the second floor (US third floor)
2 on the ground floor (US first floor)
3 on the third floor (US fourth floor)
4 on the ground floor (US first floor)
5 on the third floor (US fourth floor)
6 on the ground floor (US first floor)
7 on the third floor (US fourth floor)
8 on the second floor (US third floor)
9 on the first floor (US second floor)
10 on the third floor (US fourth floor)

157

1 It's eleven thousand and nineteen kilometres from Sydney
to Johannesburg.
2 It's eighteen thousand, three hundred and forty kilometres
from Tokyo to Buenos Aires.
3 It's nine thousand and sixty-seven kilometres from London
to Johannesburg.
4 It's sixteen thousand and three kilometres from New York
to Sydney.

5 It's nine thousand, five hundred and eighty-four kilometres
from London to Tokyo.
6 It's ten thousand, eight hundred and sixty-nine kilometres
from Tokyo to New York.
7 It's eight thousand, one hundred and nine kilometres from
Johannesburg to Buenos Aires.
8 It's seven thousand, eight hundred and twelve kilometres
from Sydney to Tokyo.
9 It's eleven thousand, one hundred and twenty-nine
kilometres from Buenos Aires to London.

158

1 The cheque number is seven double oh, two oh seven.
The account number is one two one two one two one two.
The bank branch number is two oh nine nine nine three.
The cheque is for one hundred and ninety-three pounds.
The cheque is dated the thirtieth of August, nineteen
eighty-five. The cheque is payable to Mister P. Smith and
is signed by J.M. England.
2 one thousand, one hundred and twenty-two pounds; one
hundred and twenty-seven pounds; one thousand, two
hundred and one pounds; two thousand, one hundred
and thirty-five pounds; three thousand, one hundred and
ten pounds.

159

Japan produces four point five million cars and three point
eight million motorbikes a year.
The USA produces two point three million lorries and six
point five million cars a year.
The USSR produces nought point eight million lorries and
one point one million motorbikes a year.
The UK produces nought point four million lorries a year.
France produces three point one million cars and one million
motorbikes a year.
West Germany produces three million cars a year.
Italy produces nought point eight million motorbikes a year.

160

(Possible answers)
I think Mary weighs about seventy-five kilos.
I think Julia weighs about fifty-two kilos.
I think Bob weighs about eighty kilos.
I think Sally weighs about thirty kilos.
I think the father's about six feet two inches tall (six foot two).
I think the mother's about five feet six inches tall (five foot
six).
I think the daughter's about four feet six inches tall (four foot
six).
I think the son's about three feet ten inches tall (three foot
ten).

161

(Possible answers)
On average, a four-year-old girl is one metre three
centimetres tall and weighs sixteen point six kilos. A four-
year-old boy weighs sixteen point eight kilos and is one
metre four centimetres tall, etc.

162

(Possible answers)
2 I'd like the electric one/the manual one.
3 I'd like the fast one/the slow one.
4 I'd like the big one/the small one.
5 I'd like the fresh ones/the tinned ones.
6 I'd like the cheaper one/the more expensive one.
7 I'd like the English ones/the French ones.
8 I'd like the old one/the modern one.
9 I'd like the ones with stripes/the ones without stripes.

10 I'd like the round one/the square one.

11 I'd like the chocolate ones/the plain ones.

163

(Possible answers)

1 You ought to lie down/stay at home. You oughtn't to go to work.

2 You ought to see a doctor.

3 You ought to have your eyes tested.

4 You ought to go to the dentist's. You oughtn't to eat so many sweet things.

5 You ought to set the alarm-clock/go to bed early. You oughtn't to stay up too late tonight.

6 You ought to eat less/go on a diet/get more exercise. You oughtn't to eat so many fatty foods.

7 You ought to ask him for it. You oughtn't to lend him money again.

8 You ought to have/get it renewed.

164

(Suggestions)

I ought to have visited my aunt. I ought to have finished a report. I ought to have rung up my brother. etc.

165

1 room of his own 2 flat of her own 3 house/home of their own 4 of my own 5 of their own 6 car of our own 7 of his own 8 of his own 9 of her own 10 business of our own

166

1 frightening 2 tired 3 frightened 4 exciting 5 excited 6 confusing 7 confused 8 tiring 9 interesting 10 boring 11 bored 12 interested

167

(Possible answers)

1 Not knowing who he was, I didn't speak to him.

2 She sat watching the rain for hours.

3 Needing some fresh air, I went jogging in the woods.

4 After leaving you, I went to the post office.

5 Before leaving on holiday, always make sure that the doors and windows are locked.

6 All the people queueing over there are hoping to get tickets for the football match.

7 If properly looked after, the engine will do another twenty thousand miles at least.

8 Being rich, he could afford a big house in the country.

9 Looking at the menu, I found that the prices had gone up again.

10 Not being in a hurry, I decided to walk to the office.

11 Taking a taxi, he managed to get to the station on time.

12 Who's that woman talking to the postman?

168

(Possible answers)

Coffee is grown in Brazil.

Gold is mined in South Africa.

Maize is grown in the USA.

Rice is grown in China and India.

Ships are built in Japan.

Silk is produced in Japan and China.

Tea is grown in India.

Televisions and radios are manufactured in Japan and in the USA.

Tin is mined in Malaysia and in the USSR.

Wine is produced in France.

Wool is produced in Australia.

169

1 is harvested 2 is taken 3 is ground 4 is mixed 5 is cut 6 are shaped 7 are placed 8 are put 9 is taken 10 is left 11 is sliced 12 is packed 13 is delivered

170

(Possible answers)

2 The eggs are being collected.

3 The corn is being harvested.

4 The field is being ploughed.

5 The cows are being milked.

6 The milk is being collected.

7 The stable is being cleaned out.

8 The pigs are being fed.

9 The tractor is being repaired.

10 The barn is being painted.

11 The ducks are being fed.

171

(Possible answers)

2 I think the Empire State Building was built in 1930.

3 I think the Colosseum of Rome was begun in the 1st century AD.

4 I think the Great Wall of China was begun in the 3rd century BC.

5 I think the Capitol was completed in 1865.

6 I think the Pyramids of Gizeh were built between 2690 and 2560 BC.

172

'1984' was written by George Orwell.

The 'Mona Lisa' was painted by Leonardo da Vinci.

The telephone was invented by Alexander Bell.

'Robinson Crusoe' was written by Daniel Defoe.

Penicillin was discovered by Alexander Fleming.

Radioactivity was discovered by Becquerel.

'West Side Story' was composed by Leonard Bernstein.

'Madame Butterfly' was composed by Giacomo Puccini.

Dynamite was invented by Alfred Nobel.

'The Old Guitarist' was painted by Picasso.

173

(Suggestions)

A new hospital has been built in our town. Industry has been developed. Housing has been modernized. New laws have been made. The public transport system has been improved. etc.

174

(Possible answers)

I don't think talking robots will have been invented.

I think international traffic laws will have been introduced.

I think a cure for cancer will have been found.

I don't think passenger transport to the moon will have been introduced.

I think a European currency will have been introduced.

I don't think the world's hunger problems will have been solved.

I don't think supersonic trains will have been invented.

I think new energy sources will have been found.

I don't think the problem of world peace will have been solved.

I think satellite TV for everyone will have been introduced.

175

(Possible answers)

The Rex Cinema is going to be replaced by an office block.

A bank is going to be put up in Wood Street.

The Grand Hotel is going to be replaced by a supermarket.

New houses are going to be put up in George Street.
Rose Street is going to be widened.
Trees are going to be planted on both sides of Rose Street.
The bus station is going to be moved to South Street.
The park is going to be made bigger.
A restaurant is going to be built in the park.
A swimming pool and shops are going to be built in West Street.
The old houses in West Street are going to be pulled down.
A hospital is going to be built in South Street.
The old houses between North Street and West Street are going to be replaced by a green area with trees.
A post office is going to be built in North Street.
New shops are going to be put up in North Street.

176

1 were 2 were 3 hunted 4 brought 5 had
6 crept 7 killed 8 used 9 ate 10 made 11 built
12 stayed 13 collected 14 played 15 fought

177

(Possible answers)
Flames were coming out of the upstairs windows.
Several people were standing at the windows.
Crowds of people were watching.
The police were holding back the crowds.
The firemen were trying to put out the fire with hosepipes.
Two firemen were climbing up the ladder.
One fireman was carrying a baby.
Two ambulance men were carrying someone on a stretcher.
One man was climbing down a rope.

178

(Possible answers)
2 She's cut her finger.
3 He's broken his glasses.
4 They've got married.
5 He's hurt his leg.
6 She's lost weight.
7 The car has overturned.
8 He's won the race.
9 They've robbed a bank.
10 He's broken his arm.
11 He's fallen.
12 He's knocked him out.
13 They've bought a new car.
14 He's made a cake.

179

(Possible answers)
I've never won a large sum of money. I've already bought a new car. I haven't seen a house on fire. I've always wanted to have my fortune told. I've never fallen in love. I've always wanted to eat in a famous restaurant.

180

(Possible answers)
2 They've been shopping.
3 She's been writing letters.
4 He's been repairing his car.
5 They've been fighting.
6 She's been washing her hair.
7 He's been cleaning the floor.
8 They've been playing tennis.
9 She's been hanging out the washing.
10 He's been running/jogging.
11 They've been fishing.

181

1 After day 13, China had won 15 gold medals.
2 After day 14, West Germany had won 17 gold medals.
3 After day 13, the USA had won 63 gold medals.
4 After day 13, the USA had won 53 silver medals.
5 After day 13, Romania had won 14 silver medals.

6 After day 13, China had won 7 silver medals.
7 After day 14, the USA had won 80 gold medals.
8 After day 14, Romania had won 17 bronze medals.
9 After day 15, the USA had won 83 gold medals.
10 After day 15, Romania had won 20 gold medals.
11 After day 15, West Germany had won 17 gold medals.
12 After day 15, the USA had won 61 silver medals.

182

(Possible answers)
Simon is Helen and Jim's son, Hilary's husband, Sally's brother, Paul's brother-in-law, Susie's father, Ben's uncle.
Jim is Helen's husband, Simon and Sally's father, Hilary and Paul's father-in-law, Susie and Ben's grandfather.
Sally is Helen and Jim's daughter, Paul's wife, Simon's sister, Hilary's sister-in-law, Ben's mother, Susie's aunt.
Paul is Helen and Jim's son-in-law, Sally's husband, Simon's brother-in-law, Ben's father, Susie's uncle.
Ben is Sally and Paul's son, Helen and Jim's grandson, Susie's cousin, Hilary and Simon's nephew.

183

1 Hat number one is the chef's.
2 Hat number two is Pierre's.
3 Hat number three is the rider's.
4 Hat number four is Mr Magic's.
5 Hat number five is Mr Parker's.
6 Hat number six is Tony's.
7 Hat number seven is Dusty's.
8 Hat number eight is Wilhelm's.
9 Hat number nine is Miss Smith's.

184

She's been to the greengrocer's.
She's been to the baker's.
She's been to the chemist's.
She's been to the travel agent's.
She's been to the florist's.
She's been to the grocer's.
She's been to the jeweller's.
She's been to the newsagent's.
She's been to the stationer's.
She's been to the optician's.

185

(Possible answers)
1 Yes, he's a colleague of his.
2 Yes, they are neighbours of hers.
3 Yes, he's a friend of hers.
4 Yes, she's a neighbour of hers.
5 She's a neighbour of the Hills' and a friend of Kathy's.
6 He's a colleague of John's and a friend of Kathy's.
7 Lucy is a neighbour of Kathy's.
8 They are neighbours of Mary's.
9 No, she's a neighbour of theirs.
10 No, she's a friend of his.

186

1 Yes, they're hers.
2 Yes, it's his.
3 Yes, they're theirs.
4 No, it isn't his.
5 No, it isn't hers.
6 No, it isn't theirs.
7 Yes, it's his.
8 No, it isn't hers.
9 No, they aren't his.
10 No, it isn't theirs.

187

(Possible answers)
1 You need a broom to sweep with.
2 You need a bucket to put/carry water in.

3 You need a jug to pour from.
4 You need an envelope to post a letter in.
5 You need a pillow to sleep on.
6 You need a frame to put a picture/photograph in.
7 You need a push-chair to push a baby in.
8 You need a lighter to light a cigarette with.
9 You need a suitcase to put clothes in.
10 You need a dustbin to put rubbish in.
11 You need a compass to find the direction with.
12 You need a sunshade to sit under.

188
(Possible answers)
 1 No, I never drop litter.
 2 Yes, I sometimes spend too much money on clothes.
 3 Yes, I sometimes have the radio on too loud.
 4 No, I never neglect my job.
 5 Yes, I sometimes criticize my boss behind his back.
 6 Yes, I sometimes tell little white lies.
 7 No, I never ignore a traffic light.
 8 Yes, I sometimes forget my good manners.
 9 Yes, I sometimes think more of myself than of others.
10 No, I never forget to pay my debts.

189
(Possible answers)
2 Kathy and Mike are hanging wallpaper.
3 Sue is sewing.
4 Jerry is giving a tennis lesson.
5 Sally and Ben are cooking.
6 David is playing his guitar.
7 Jill is mowing the lawn/cutting the grass.
8 Barry is painting.
9 Diana is washing her car.

190
(Suggestions)
I'm sorry it's so noisy, but we're putting up new cupboards/
but the children are playing with the dog/but the joiner's
repairing the shelves.
I'm sorry it's so untidy, but my brother's six children are
staying with us/but I'm going through some old papers/but
we're having a children's birthday party.

191
(Possible answers)
 1 is always making trouble for others.
 2 is always doing what's best for himself.
 3 is always dropping things or knocking things over.
 4 is always telling lies.
 5 is always imagining that he's ill.
 6 is always talking about other people.
 7 is always spoiling other people's fun/enjoyment.
 8 is always expecting the worst to happen.
 9 is always admiring himself/herself.
10 is always telling other people's secrets.

192
(Possible answers)
 1 When did you arrive?
 2 How long are you staying here?
 3 How did you travel?
 4 Where are you staying?
 5 Is it your first time here?
 6 Do you like it here?
 7 Have you already seen the . . . (any building)?
 8 Can you speak our language?
 9 Do you like the food here?
10 Have you been to . . . (any town)?

193
 1 You're a computer specialist, aren't you?
 2 You have been to our country before, haven't you?
 3 You are staying here for three months, aren't you?
 4 You work for an American company, don't you?
 5 You used to work for an English company, didn't you?
 6 You know a few words of our language, don't you?
 7 You would like to learn the language properly, wouldn't you?
 8 You were on holiday in our country last year, weren't you?
 9 You don't like the food very much, do you?
10 You can play tennis very well, can't you?

194
(Possible answers)
 1 No, I never iron my clothes myself./Yes, I sometimes/ always iron my clothes myself.
 2 Yes, my father hardly ever repairs the car himself./No, my husband always repairs the car himself.
 3 Yes, I always shop for food myself./No, I hardly ever shop for food myself.
 4 Yes, we decorate our flat ourselves./No, we don't decorate the house ourselves.
 5 Yes, my parents clean their house themselves./No, my parents don't clean their house themselves.
 6 Yes, I wash my clothes myself./No, I don't wash my clothes myself.
 7 Yes, my wife hardly ever does her hair herself./No, my girlfriend always does her hair herself.
 8 Yes, my father repairs things in the house himself./No, my husband hardly ever repairs things in the house himself.
 9 Yes, we wash the car ourselves./No, we don't usually wash the car ourselves.
10 Yes, my wife made the curtains herself./No, my mother didn't make the curtains herself.

195
Terry's the girl who went to Oxford University.
Susie's the girl who never did her homework.
Ted's the boy who could run a mile in five minutes.
Dan's the boy who was always in trouble.
Eric and Walter are the brothers who went to live in Malaysia.
Peter's the boy who wanted to become an actor.
Maria's the girl who spoke three languages.
Charlotte's the girl who studied medicine.
Jim's the boy who always got the best exam results.
Polly's the girl who could play three instruments.

196
(Possible answers)
 1 The tiny country that lies in the middle of Italy is San Marino.
 2 The part of China that is leased to Britain until 1997 is Hong Kong.
 3 The Danish island that lies in the Arctic is Greenland.
 4 The country that has more coastline than any other country is Canada.
 5 The city that has the world's largest football stadium is Rio de Janeiro.
 6 The island that lies at the southern point of India is Sri Lanka.
 7 The country that has the highest waterfall in the world is Venezuela.
 8 The country that covers a sixth of all the land in the world is the USSR.
 9 The city that was built specially to be a new capital about 30 years ago is Brasilia.
10 The country that has the most languages is India.

197
(Possible answers)
1 Who's the man whose tie is undone?
2 Who's the man whose glasses are falling off his nose?
3 Who's the man whose pipe's on fire?
4 Who's the man whose jacket is too tight?
5 Who's the man whose trousers are too short?
6 Who's the man whose shoes have holes in them?

198
(Possible answers)
1 The bathroom is the room you wash in.
2 The dining room is the room you eat in.
3 The kitchen is the room you prepare food in.
4 The sitting room is the room you sit in/spend leisure time in.
5 The study is the room you work in.
6 The nursery is the room the children sleep and play in.
7 The guest room is the room guests sleep in.
8 The attic is the place you store things.
9 The cellar is also a place you store/keep things.
10 The garage is the place you keep the car.

199
(Possible answers)
She wrote that she could get married at 16, but that she couldn't vote until she was 18.
She wrote that at the cinema she already paid for an adult ticket, but that she was not allowed to see adult films.
She wrote that she could drive a car at 17, but on the bus and tube she started paying adult fares at 15.
She wrote that travel companies and many airlines offered reductions for children under 12.
She wrote that the age when she became an adult seemed to depend on where she was sitting.

200
(Possible answers)
Pat Swindon said that she was glad that seat-belts had become compulsory, and that she was sure that the number of road deaths would drop.
Bill Brown said that he hated wearing a seat-belt, that he didn't feel free. He said that he didn't intend to use it in future, and that he just hoped that he didn't get caught by the police.
Patrick Marshall said that he was in favour of wearing seat-belts, and that he always fastened his. He said he always had done and he always would do.
Jane Wilson said that she saw what terrible accidents happened to people who didn't wear seat-belts. She said she hoped that belts for the back seats would also become compulsory.

201
(Possible answers)
Pam E. wants to know how she can get her boyfriend to stop smoking.
John K. wants to know whether he should tell his teacher that he's fallen in love with her.
David B. wants to know when he can legally leave home.
Barry G. wants to know why his girlfriend tells him lies.
Kathy P. wants to know whether she should marry a man who's thirty years older than herself.
Mary M. wants to know how she can get rid of her spots.
Roger A. wants to know why he hasn't made any friends at his new school.
Lucy L. wants to know why people treat her like a child.
Patricia H. wants to know whether she should go to a party with her boss.

Diana B. wants to know whether she has to give back her engagement ring.

202
2 He wants to know why it rains.
3 He wants to know why it is hotter in summer.
4 He wants to know how trees grow.
5 He wants to know why the moon only shines at night.
6 He wants to know how mountains were made.
7 He wants to know why volcanoes erupt.
8 He wants to know where rainbows come from.
9 He wants to know why there is more daylight in summer.
10 He wants to know why it thunders.
11 He wants to know why the seasons change.

203
(Possible answers)
1 I would advise him to stop smoking immediately.
2 I would tell him to go for long walks in the country at the weekends.
3 I would tell her to go to bed early.
4 I would ask him to speak more clearly.
5 I would ask her to turn the music down.
6 I would tell her to take it back to the shop.
7 I would ask her to check the bill and give me more change.
8 I would ask them to play quietly because I couldn't sleep.
9 I would advise him to take a holiday.
10 I would advise her to take it to the police station.

204
(Suggestions)
We live in the same village. He goes to the same sports club as I do. She doesn't wear the same kind of clothes as I do. We don't have the same interests. He isn't the same age. We have the same friends. We are the same height.

205
(Possible answers)
2 Shall I help you across?
3 Shall I get a doctor?
4 Shall I help you to look?
5 Shall I carry your bags?
6 Shall I hold the door open for you?
7 Shall I call the police?
8 Shall I get you some/an aspirin?

206
1 Yes, they do. 2 No, there aren't. 3 No, it doesn't.
4 Yes, they do. 5 Yes, it has. 6 Yes, there is. 7 Yes, it does. 8 No, there isn't. 9 Yes, they have. 10 Yes, there is. 11 Yes, they do. 12 No, there isn't.

207
1 Yes, I am./No, I'm not.   6 Yes, I do./No, I don't.
2 Yes, I have./No, I haven't.   7 Yes, I am./No, I'm not.
3 Yes, I do./No, I don't.   8 Yes, I am./No, I'm not.
4 Yes, I have./No, I haven't.   9 Yes, I did./No, I didn't.
5 Yes, I do.   10 Yes, I was./No, I wasn't.

208
(Possible answers)
The washing machine shouldn't be in the attic. It should be in the kitchen.
The dishwasher shouldn't be in the bedroom. It should be in the kitchen.
The dining table shouldn't be in the bedroom. It should be in the living room.

The bed shouldn't be in the study. It should be in the bedroom.
The typewriter shouldn't be in the bathroom. It should be in the study.
The telephone shouldn't be in the bathroom. It should be in the hall or in the living room.
The wardrobe shouldn't be in the living room. It should be in the bedroom.
The saucepans shouldn't be in the living room. They should be in the kitchen.
The cooker shouldn't be in the hall. It should be in the kitchen.
The sofa shouldn't be in the hall. It should be in the living room.
The bicycle shouldn't be in the kitchen. It should be in the garage.
The television shouldn't be in the kitchen. It should be in the living room.
The armchair shouldn't be in the garage. It should be in the living room.
The pictures shouldn't be in the garage. They should be in the living room.

209
(Possible answers)
1 You shouldn't eat so many sweets.
2 You should ring the lost property office or the police station.
3 You should sell it and buy a new one.
4 You shouldn't eat so much.
5 You should spend less money on clothes.
6 You should try to get a new job as soon as possible.
7 You shouldn't give her your money.
8 You should take it back to the record shop.

210
(Suggestions)
3 I've known my best friend's family since they invited me to their house a year ago.
4 I've known my class teacher since he started teaching at our school.
5 I've known my English teacher since I began learning English.
6 I've known my girlfriend since last March.
7 I've known my doctor since I came to this town.
8 I've known my dentist since I was a child.
9 I've known my butcher since he opened his shop last year.

211
(Possible answers)
1 bunch of grapes, 1 basket of strawberries, 1 lb. of cherries, 5 lb. of potatoes, 1 basket of raspberries, 2 lb. of tomatoes, 1 bunch of radishes, 4 large peaches, 3 large oranges, 2 lb. of apples

212
(Possible answers)
1 I think so. I'm afraid not.
2 I'm afraid so. I don't think so.
3 I hope not. I suppose so.
4 I don't think so. I'm afraid so.
5 I hope not. I don't believe so.
6 I hope so. I expect so.
7 I'm afraid not. I think so.
8 I think so. I hope so.
9 I'm afraid not. I suppose so.
10 I don't believe so. I don't think so.
11 I believe so. I suppose so. I'm afraid not.
12 I hope so. I believe so. I don't expect so. I don't suppose so.

213
(Possible answers)
Susan was born in 1964. So was Diana.

Mary is from Scotland. So is Susan.
Diana writes shorthand at 100 words per minute. So does Susan.
Diana types at 50 words per minute. So does Mary.
Susan has been a shorthand typist for 4 years. So has Diana.
Diana likes cooking. So does Susan.
Diana likes reading. So do Mary and Susan.
Mary likes dancing. So does Susan.
Diana can play tennis. So can Susan.
Susan can swim well. So can Mary.

214
(Possible answers)
There's some fruit/coffee.
There are some biscuits/bread rolls.
There isn't any beer/wine/ice-cream.
There aren't any peanuts/cigarettes.
There's hardly any mineral water/orange juice/cake.
There are hardly any sandwches/sausages.

215
1 anywhere, somewhere   2 somebody, anybody
3 anything, anything   4 something, anywhere
5 anything   6 Somebody   7 somewhere
8 somewhere   9 anybody   10 anywhere

216
1 yet, still   2 already   3 yet, yet   4 already   5 yet, still
6 already   7 already, yet, still   8 already, yet   9 yet, still   10 yet, still

217
(Possible answers)
I like Helen and she likes me.
Bill likes me, but I don't like him.
Simon and I like Lucy, but she doesn't like us.
Cathy likes Simon, but he doesn't like her.
Bill likes Cathy, but she doesn't like him.
Helen and Alison like Tim, but he doesn't like them.
Bill and George like Helen and Alison, but they don't like them.

218
1 such   2 so   3 such   4 such   5 such   6 such
7 so   8 so   9 so   10 so

219
(Suggestions)
1 It takes me about twenty minutes.
2 It takes me ages./It doesn't take me long.
3 It takes me about 8 minutes.
4 It doesn't take more than half an hour.
5 It takes about 2 minutes.
6 The journey to work took about twenty minutes./The walk to school took me about ten minutes.
7 The last exercise took me about five minutes./The last exercise didn't take me long.
8 Breakfast this morning took about a quarter of an hour.
9 My morning shower took me about 5 minutes.
10 It took me/I took a few years to learn to pronounce English well.

220
(Suggestions)
1 I usually get up at a quarter past six (six fifteen) during the week.
2 On Sundays, I don't get up until nine o'clock.
3 I go to bed at about a quarter to ten (nine forty-five) during the week.

4 I don't go to bed until about midnight at the weekend.
5 I have breakfast at a quarter to seven (six forty-five).
6 I usually leave home at about half past eight (eight thirty) in the morning.
7 I arrive home from work at six o'clock.
8 On Sundays we have lunch at half past two (two thirty).
9 I have my evening meal about eight o'clock.
10 I usually watch the news on television at a quarter to six (five forty-five).

221
(Possible answers)
1 Are there windmills in Egypt? No, there aren't, but there are pyramids in Egypt.
2 Are there kiwis in China? No, there aren't, but there are pandas in China.
3 Are there kangaroos near the River Amazon? No, there aren't, but there are alligators near the River Amazon.
4 Is there tea in Brazil? No, there isn't, but there's coffee in Brazil.
5 Are there pyramids in Holland? No, there aren't, but there are windmills in Holland.
6 Is there iron in Iran? No, there isn't, but there's oil in Iran.
7 Are there diamonds in Sweden? No, there aren't, but there's iron in Sweden.
8 Are there alligators in Australia? No, there aren't, but there are kangaroos in Australia.
9 Are there pandas in New Zealand? No, there aren't, but there are kiwis in New Zealand.
10 Is there oil in South Africa? No, there isn't, but there are diamonds in South Africa.

222
1 until 2 by 3 until 4 by 5 To 6 to/until 7 to/until 8 by 9 until 10 by, until

223
(Possible answers)
There used to be a post office in Duke Street. Now it's a bank.
There used to be a petrol station in Queen Street. Now there's a hotel.
There used to be a park. Now it's a car park and shopping centre.
There didn't use to be a school in Church Street.
There didn't use to be a post office in West Street.
There didn't use to be a telephone box in West Street.
There didn't use to be a bus stop in Queen Street.
There didn't use to be a telephone box next to the church.
There didn't use to be a shopping centre in King Street.

224
(Suggestions)
I'm used to living in a big city/working hard/walking long distances/spending a lot of time alone/travelling abroad a lot.
I'm not used to eating spicy foods/going to bed late/lying in the sun for hours/looking after small children/riding a bicycle.

225
(Suggestions)
I sent my aunt a big bouquet of flowers on her last birthday. I gave my father a new pipe for Christmas.

226
1 If 2 if 3 when 4 whether 5 If 6 if/whether 7 whether/if 8 If 9 If, if 10 When

227
1 Whatever 2 Whenever 3 wherever/whenever
4 wherever 5 Whoever 6 however 7 whichever
8 Whenever 9 wherever 10 whoever

228
Kate wishes she hadn't bought so many new clothes.
She wishes she could handle money.
She wishes she spoke a foreign language.
She wishes she hadn't wasted so much time at school.
She wishes she hadn't spent all her savings.
She wishes she took life seriously.
She wishes she had got a steady boyfriend.
She wishes Paul had asked her out.
Paul wishes he had gone to university.
He wishes he had become a teacher.
He wishes he had worked harder at school.
He wishes he had got a car.
He wishes he could dance.
He wishes he wasn't shy.
He wishes he made friends easily.
He wishes he was interested in sport.
He wishes he had dared to ask Kate out.

229
(Possible answers)
1 It's worth seeing.
2 They aren't worth mending/keeping.
3 They are worth collecting.
4 It's worth keeping.
5 It's worth reading.
6 They aren't worth buying.
7 It's worth visiting.
8 It's worth working for.
9 They aren't worth keeping.
10 It's worth listening to.

230
(Possible answers)
1 I'd rather you took life more seriously.
2 I'd rather you didn't wear old jeans all the time.
3 I'd rather you didn't buy so many presents.
4 I'd rather you didn't work on Saturdays.
5 I'd rather you had your hair cut.
6 I'd rather you didn't drive so fast.
7 I'd rather you didn't criticize my friends.
8 I'd rather you stopped spending money on clothes.
9 I'd rather you didn't waste so much time on the phone.
10 I'd rather you worked a bit harder.